IMPERMANENCE
IN PLAIN ENGLISH

IMPERMANENCE
IN PLAIN ENGLISH

*Bhante Gunaratana
and Julia Harris*

Wisdom

Wisdom Publications
132 Perry Street
New York, NY 10014 USA
wisdomexperience.org

Library of Congress Cataloging-in-Publication Data
Names: Gunaratana, Henepola, 1927– author. | Harris, Julia, author.
Title: Impermanence in plain English / Bhante Gunaratana and Julia Harris.
Description: First edition. | New York: Wisdom Publications, 2023. |
    Includes bibliographical references.
Identifiers: LCCN 2023012279 (print) | LCCN 2023012280 (ebook) |
    ISBN 9781614298915 (paperback) | ISBN 9781614299042 (ebook)
Subjects: LCSH: Impermanence (Buddhism) | Buddhism—Doctrines.
Classification: LCC BQ4261 .G86 2023 (print) | LCC BQ4261 (ebook) |
    DDC 294.3/42—dc23/eng/20230503
LC record available at https://lccn.loc.gov/2023012279
LC ebook record available at https://lccn.loc.gov/2023012280

ISBN 978-1-61429-891-5   ebook ISBN 978-1-61429-904-2

27 26 25 24 23
5 4 3 2 1

Cover design by Phil Pascuzzo. Interior design by Gopa & Ted 2.

Printed on acid-free paper that meets the guidelines for permanence and durability of
the Production Guidelines for Book Longevity of the Council on Library Resources.

Printed in the United States of America.

Please visit fscus.org.

Contents

Preface: Come and See

I AM A NINETY-FIVE-YEAR-OLD MONK. By now, I have come to see life as a dream. Fifty years ago, I wrote a paper for a first-year English class at American University that offered a basic framework for meditation in my tradition, the Theravada school of Buddhism. The paper was called "Come and See." In the oldest set of texts attributable to the Buddha, and in the daily chanting of monks like me, the Pali term *ehipassiko* means just that; *ehi* is an invitation to come, and *passiko* is one who sees. We practice looking inward in ways that give rise to liberating insight. These insights are said to be known individually by those who are wise.

Since that time, I have looked within. I have seen, heard, smelled, tasted, touched, and thought countless sights, sounds, smells, tangibles, and thoughts. All of them are gone. In their place remains peace. I am at home with impermanence. I want to convey this awareness to you in a way that can be understood directly. This book shares the same spirit of "come and see" as that paper fifty years ago, but the focus is different. I wish for you to taste the fruit of meditation firsthand. These pages invite you to join me in the personal experience of impermanence, for it is there that you will find wisdom and freedom.

Bhante Henepola Gunaratana
The Bhavana Society
2022

A Note on Language

THIS BOOK UTILIZES words from the Pali Canon, ancient texts ascribed to the Buddha, written down from an oral tradition that for hundreds of years after his passing was the only method of preserving his words. These verses are like a road map or a driver's manual to the experience of freedom.

Pali is a technical language for Buddhist meditation training, conveying some concepts in ways that English cannot. While words that might be new to the reader or those that play a significant methodological role will appear in italics at their first use, words in popular usage will be left as is, such as *Buddha*, here denoting the enlightened being born as Siddhattha Gotama (or, in Sanskrit, Siddhartha Gautama); *Dhamma*, the teachings of that buddha or the natural law of all things, sometimes meaning "phenomena"; and *Sangha*, in this case referring to the community of enlightened Buddhist monastics. Other concepts such as *bhikkhu*, the term for monk, and *sutta*, a teaching discourse, will be used interchangeably with their English counterparts as appropriate.

Regarding citations, all quotations from the classical texts are translated by the authors unless otherwise noted. Diacritics have been omitted from these for ease of reading. In many other cases we use translations by Bhikkhu Bodhi; for those, we have included diacritics out of respect and gratitude for his work. Although the translated passages contained in this book might seem repetitive, please remember that this stylistic aspect of the texts helped monks with memorization, so as to keep the teachings alive during the hundreds of years before writing became available, and importantly, it will also remind contemporary readers to place their attention precisely in very specific ways, over and over again, a process that is necessary to achieve the goal of meditation. Practicing with the Pali in this way will make juicy and rich that which might otherwise seem dry or monotonous. It is hoped that the reader will encounter great benefit from contemplation according to these timeless instructions.

Introduction:
Protections for the Heart

TOGETHER we are about to embark on a journey into unknown territory. We might call our investigation *ajjhattanupassana*: contemplation (*anupassati*) of the deeply personal, peculiar to the subjective, and of that which originates from within (*ajjhatta*), a method of observation that can ultimately prove liberating. By engaging sincerely in this practice of introspection, we will perceive much sensory data and myriad mental formations. As we refine our practice toward freedom, the sheer quantity of happenings in the mental world as well as the rate of our knowing them will seem to quicken. But we don't need to be overwhelmed by this; the Buddha's teachings offer protections for our minds and hearts, so that both now and at the time of death we can rest at ease with the intensification of uncertainty. The Dhamma points to ease in ways of attention that are not dependent upon having ideal conditions in an unpredictable world.

The wise ruler, said the Buddha, knows that safety lies not in building walls against danger but in removing fortifications of the heart, so that unwholesomeness cannot find any foothold in the first place. In traversing this inner terrain, rather than amassing arms, he declared it best to generate reserves of wholesome mental states for protection. The training exercises he recommended are collectively called the Four Foundations of Mindfulness. This is the placement of careful attention on and in this very body, these feelings, this mind, and on the objects of mind respectively. "That is your home," he said. "Reside in this home. As you dwell in the ancestral abode, Mara will not attack you."[1]

On more than one occasion, the Buddha roused his students, "Monks, be islands unto yourselves; be a refuge unto yourselves with no other refuge. Let the Dhamma be your island; let the Dhamma be your refuge, with no other refuge."[2] In his entire lifetime, he did not find the shelter of any place or person to be more effective than the sensibly cultivated heart and mind.

Of course, the Buddha did consider it important to have a teacher for guidance and respect; it was just that he could not find any more skilled and wise than himself.[3] We can look within and find that teacher, too. The Buddha did not appoint any person as successor. Just before his passing, he exhorted his followers to work out their own deliverance from stress by following the Dhamma itself as a guide.

By Dhamma, he meant the nature of things just as they are, not subject to manipulation or elaboration by the mind. "Let me then honor, respect, and dwell in dependence on this very Dhamma to which I have fully awakened,"[4] said the Buddha soon after his full liberation from suffering. Even though he was fully enlightened and had seen the Dhamma in himself; even though he had perfected his morality, concentration, wisdom, and liberation, as well as the vision and knowledge of total release from suffering, still he continued to live in accordance with Dhamma. "One who sees Dhamma . . . sees me; one who sees me, sees Dhamma. Truly seeing Dhamma, one sees me; seeing me, one sees Dhamma."[5]

This is a practical book about touching impermanence with simplicity—about how to enter into the direct, felt sense of living impermanence, free from all thought and cognition. It might sound quite nice to experience such a fundamental teaching for ourselves. Yet profound change is all-pervading and unrelenting. If all things are inherently unstable, how can we find resort in anything? A person is changing. I am changing; you are changing. Conditions all around us and inside of us are changing. But we don't need to be disconcerted. Reality has always been this way. We are simply coming to see things as they are.

In fact, there is space all around and within, if we turn the mind to notice. Meanwhile, wholesome aspirations can help us to ride the waves of change, until we find a peace that is open and free. Our temporary shelter is the resting of attention directly on the personal body, in the body; on the personal feelings, in the feelings; and so forth, with nothing to do, nothing to compel thoughts outward. As we clarify our understanding of change through this project of exploration, our sense of what constitutes safety will also change. Eventually, the awakened heart will come to reflect its matured qualities, with a responsiveness that knows security everywhere.

The Buddha, Dhamma, and Sangha are functional ideals that support and cannot complicate our situation. For the Buddha, there remained not a single dark corner in his mind. He had swept out and examined all aspects of view until none remained fixed. His enlightenment was so perfect that he saw all beings purely, flawlessly, without any shade of a doubt as to the workings of becoming—as to how our minds give rise to how things are in each moment.

This is akin to seeing every single object in the field of awareness with utterly clear eyesight. His perception was as astute and unobstructed as the sunrise on a cloudless autumn day marked only by the vastness and clarity of the sky. He saw no self anywhere, so there were no corners in which dust could settle, or surfaces upon which it might accumulate. There were no edges.

The Dhamma consists of the intention to not harm plus the instructions leading to insight. It is said that one who stays with Dhamma stays with the Buddha—these words steer us toward the real refuge within ourselves.

The Sangha, or community of awakening beings, expands our sense of possibility and lends solidarity. We are reminded that there are indeed beings in this very world who practice in just this way, aspiring toward the conduct of the Buddha, in accordance with Dhamma. So too, we find inspiration in meeting fellow meditators whose practice has borne fruit.

While growing into familiarity with these ideas, think big. By taking refuge in what is timeless, it is possible to approach the deathless and to reside beyond Mara's reach; the thought of the Buddha protects you.

Who is this Mara? What is the force that Mara represents? This character is the personification of distraction: any temptation that beckons us to waste life in the mere satisfaction of compulsion. Contemplating death can help us with Mara. Can we see our own death at every moment? If so, we can restore alignment with our inner integrity. All that is required to see this truth—namely, that we are all subject to the reality of human natural history—is that we pay total attention to ourselves in the living organism of this physical body. Whether sitting, walking, standing, lying down, whenever we are awake, we die in every instant and are likewise reborn. These two activities, the living and dying of being, operate perpetually until the entire mechanism comes apart and ceases to function.

Examining reality until we see the momentary interworking of forms and ideas might seem silly or unfamiliar at first. Perhaps it is hard to see any point in meditating at all, but with sustained practice, new worlds of experience will reveal themselves. Our range of mental mobility naturally expands; we feel a sense of release.

Perhaps you ride a bicycle well. Try to teach me how to ride it. You might feel that you are hitting your head against the wall. You see how difficult it is to teach me how to ride a bicycle. I have never done this task in my entire life. When I was growing up in a most primitive rural village, nobody owned or had access to a bicycle, let alone knew how to ride one. Now, at ninety-five years of age, I ride a bicycle only in dreams. But you can ride one effortlessly without even holding on to the handlebars. How easy it is for you! It is so difficult for me. I might find it difficult to teach some people how to practice right mindfulness, even though I do it just like you ride a bicycle.

Not here, not there, not in between. That is the end of suffering. This means that every moment, every fraction of every moment, we are moving, never stopping. Mind is pedaling, propelled by momentum and compulsion. There is no fixed place, no fixed moment, nothing static; this is the advice the Buddha once gave to a man named Bahiya Daruciya in ancient India. Its efficacy remains and the result of its application is more expansive than the intellect alone can grasp. Peace can be known. What you think of as "self," that which you assume to be permanent, eternal, unchanging, and immutable, even those subtle parts that really feel like some unchanging aspect of "you," are, in fact, constantly moving. In this ephemeral body and mind, you cannot find a single fixed point. Just when you are thinking that there is such a thing, that thing is gone. You think, "It is here." Blink your eyes, and it is gone. What you thought to be true in that same instant becomes untrue.

There is a story of a beautiful girl who is dancing, singing captivating melodies on a stage. A man is going to meet her with a pot full to the brim of oil. Another man is going right after him with sword raised, ready to slice off his head if he spills even one drop of oil. This is the simile for the ardent practitioner of mindfulness. The Buddha issued an open invitation for all who sought his instruction to "come and see" how mindful that man carrying the pot of oil on his head must be. It is a simile designed to evoke the experience of things as they are in a way so potent, so direct as to liberate the heart and mind from stress. These teachings point to a knowing of impermanence that is immediate. It is established in the body with inner perception that defies mere intellectual description. Although practicing this degree of mindfulness amid sensual distraction demands diligence, the fruits of the Buddha's practice are many and profound. They are available to all who set their minds on freedom, who are intent upon discovering the impermanence, the inherent selflessness, and above all, the capacity for release from suffering that is here and now.

> "Bhikkhus, suppose that on hearing, 'The most beautiful girl of the land! The most beautiful girl of the land!' a great crowd of people would assemble. Now that most beautiful girl of the

land would dance exquisitely and sing exquisitely. On hearing, 'The most beautiful girl of the land is dancing! The most beautiful girl of the land is singing!' an even larger crowd of people would assemble. Then a man would come along, wishing to live, not wishing to die, wishing for happiness, averse to suffering. Someone would say to him: 'Good man, you must carry around this bowl of oil filled to the brim between the crowd and the most beautiful girl of the land. A man with a drawn sword will be following right behind you, and wherever you spill even a little of it, right there he will fell your head.'

"What do you think, bhikkhus, would that man stop attending to that bowl of oil and out of negligence turn his attention outward?"

"No, venerable sir."

"I have made up this simile, bhikkhus, in order to convey a meaning. This here is the meaning: 'The bowl of oil filled to the brim,' this is a designation for mindfulness directed to the body. Therefore, bhikkhus, you should train yourselves thus: 'We will develop and cultivate mindfulness directed to the body, make it our vehicle, make it our basis, stabilize it, exercise ourselves in it, and fully perfect it.' Thus, bhikkhus, should you train yourselves."[6]

We might "come and see" how difficult it is to practice mindfulness amid all kinds of commitments. Our minds run in circles and vacillate from past to future, storing and dredging up all kinds of memories, planning many futures. Keeping the mind poised on the very real impermanence that informs every fraction of the current moment can be tricky.

How do we carry the figurative vessel of oil without a single drip, when our attention can so easily become distracted by attraction and aversion? In the tradition of Theravada Buddhist meditation, one way we generate continuity of mindfulness sufficient for the touching of impermanence is by cultivating just enough concentration. This gathering of attention allows you to attend to each happening with poise and precision while simultaneously knowing a more spacious peace. These instructions are intended to guide you to that point.

CHAPTER 1

Responding to the Invitation

A SIMPLE INVITATION CAN lead to profound results for those who know how to engage wisely.

The Buddha found freedom in seeing how the mind and heart operate. In uttering *ehipassiko*, he extended the offer that we undertake the same project. He was a human being who looked inward to see things just as they are, and he trusted us to join him there. His suggestion to "come and see" is our opening to unravel the processes leading to human stress. But first, how do we reply to such a proposition?

When you receive an invitation, you ask these questions:

1. Who invites me?
2. Where should I go?
3. What will I see there?

In this case, you receive these answers:

1. Nobody invites you.
2. There's nowhere to go.
3. There's nothing to see.

We are being invited by nobody to go nowhere and see nothing? How could that be? These answers may seem puzzling, but they do make sense in the context of the Buddha's teaching. With ehipassiko, we are invited to go nowhere in the outside world but rather to turn the attention inward. The "come" of "come and see" means we should come closer to our own minds and hearts. We need not go anywhere at all; we simply look inside.

THE SIX QUALITIES OF DHAMMA

"Come and see" is one of the six qualities of the Dhamma that the Buddha taught. *Dhamma*, in his time, meant a variety of things. Here it refers to his teachings about the nature of reality, which he described as being imbued with interdependence, impermanence, and the very real possibility for liberation from suffering in this life. Aside from ehipassiko, which is traditionally listed fourth, the other qualities are "well-expounded" (*svakkhato*), "directly visible" (*sanditthiko*), "unaffected by time" (*akaliko*), "leading onward" (*opanayiko*), and "to be realized personally by the wise" (*paccattam veditabbo vinnuhi*). Monastics in my tradition chant these words for contemplation every day. Let's unpack them in order to comprehend them for ourselves.

Well-expounded: The teachings of the Buddha, for instance, the noble eightfold path and dependent origination, are not mere words; they are descriptions of interactions in time and space that are actually quite real. In addition, the practical directions for how to get a glimpse of the reality to which they point are so well described by the Buddha's teaching that when you investigate impartially in this manner, you will almost certainly find clarity and profundity in the truth of your own experience.

Directly visible: This means that we do not need anyone else to interpret the truth that we encounter within ourselves. Insights can be tested in your own body and mind.

Unaffected by time: Some of you might wonder, "How could this ancient Buddha's teaching be applied to my complicated life in this technologically advanced age?" In that case, please consider this question instead: "Once born, can we stop growth, decay, and death?" Nobody can stop these consequences of birth. This progression and deterioration is the indisputable consequence of getting a body, true from the time life began. The nature of the body is not some predicament that began after the Industrial Revolution. The Buddha's teaching addresses this fundamental question.

Leading onward: The Dhamma welcomes the seeker onto a path that is lovely right from the outset, yet this initial taste of well-being beckons us to embark on an even more rewarding journey. When we live in accordance with the recommendations of Dhamma, ultimately, we end up attaining the stateless state where birth, growth, decay, and death stop. We can obtain lasting peace.

To be realized personally by the wise: Even if we are not very wise, wisdom arises in us when we practice Dhamma. We sense something novel, something excellent in the cultivation of wisdom, and we enjoy its pursuit more than other more fleeting pleasures. As increasingly wise individuals, we will eventually realize the supreme bliss of liberation. This is something inside ourselves; nobody else can find it for us.

HOW TO LOOK, HOW TO SEE

The "see" in "come and see" refers to seeing Dhamma, the truth of how things are. We are called to investigate within ourselves what that truth is. We shine the light of our inner eye on everything and know the unfolding of our own experience to be Dhamma. All that is happening in ourselves all the time is nothing but Dhamma. Dhamma is within us. We are Dhamma.

For the purposes of this book, in order to obtain the benefit of the Buddha's instructions directly as in ancient times, you should imagine yourself receiving the instructions exactly as they are given to the monk or nun being addressed in each sutta. It is important that you investigate internally in just this way; this is the method for the hearing of Dhamma. It is the timeless way for internalizing Dhamma for its intended benefit. With that in mind, consider how the Buddha replied when the monk Upavana asked him the meaning of *ehipassiko:*

"Here, Upavāṇa, having seen a form with the eye, a bhikkhu experiences the form as well as lust for the form. He understands that lust for forms exists internally thus: 'There is in me lust for forms internally.' Since that is so, Upavāṇa, the Dhamma is directly visible, immediate, inviting one to come and see, applicable, to be personally experienced by the wise.

"Further, Upavāṇa, having heard a sound with the ear . . . [smelled an odor with the nose . . . tasted a flavor with the tongue . . . touched a tangible with the body . . .] having cognized a mental phenomenon with the mind, a bhikkhu experiences the mental phenomenon as well as lust for the mental phenomenon. He understands that lust for mental phenomena exists internally thus: 'There is in me lust for mental phenomena internally.' Since that is so, Upavāṇa, the Dhamma is directly visible, immediate, inviting one to come and see, applicable, to be personally experienced by the wise.

"But here, Upavāṇa, having seen a form with the eye, a bhikkhu experiences the form without experiencing lust for the form. He understands that lust for forms does not exist internally thus: 'There is in me no lust for forms internally.' Since that is so, Upavāṇa, the Dhamma is directly visible, immediate, inviting one to come and see, applicable, to be personally experienced by the wise.

"Further, Upavāṇa, having heard a sound with the ear . . . having cognized a mental phenomenon with the mind, a bhikkhu experiences the mental phenomenon without experiencing lust for the mental phenomenon. He understands that lust for mental phenomena does not exist internally thus: 'There is in me no lust for mental phenomena internally.' Since that is so, Upavāṇa, the Dhamma is directly visible, immediate, inviting one to come and see, applicable, to be personally experienced by the wise."[7]

Having made sure to go through each of the six sense doors—seeing, hearing, smelling, tasting, touching, and the mind—according to the refrain, you will see that these instructions are, in fact, what we do whenever we practice insight (*vipassana*) meditation: We see the workings of Dhamma within us. We do this by bringing to the fore the ways in which we relate to sensory objects, as well as to objects like thoughts in mind. We notice magnetism and repulsion, and eventually their effects on our perception of reality. It is possible to recognize what the ancients called "lust" by feeling into the mere experience of wanting or anticipation, no matter how subtle or how vague. This is part of the glue that we supply to our reality. By acknowledging that there is a feeling tone or stickiness that connects us with objects "out there," we learn to trace the attention back to where it started.

Contemplation of Mind

This process is further explained in the *Mahasatipatthana Sutta, The Greater Discourse on the Four Foundations of Mindfulness.* The third section of this sutta is called "Contemplation of Mind." After emphasizing investigation of sensory phenomena and the feeling that follows them, this passage directs the activity of inward-looking specifically toward states of mind that color perceptions.

> "Here a bhikkhu understands a mind with lust as a mind with lust; a mind without lust as a mind without lust; a mind with hatred as a mind with hatred; a mind without hatred as a mind without hatred; a mind with delusion as a mind with delusion; a mind without delusion as a mind without delusion; a contracted mind as contracted and a distracted mind as distracted; an exalted mind as exalted and an unexalted mind as unexalted; a surpassable mind as surpassable and an unsurpassable mind as unsurpassable; a concentrated mind as concentrated and an unconcentrated mind as

unconcentrated; a liberated mind as liberated and an unliberated mind as unliberated."[8]

In meditation, we can explore in real time how sense phenomena in daily life are not always recognized at face value. We notice that the raw materials of being often undergo interpretation unconsciously and immediately following contact between mental objects and the sense doors. It is crucial to see not just with the outer eye but also with the inner eye, to feel into each step of the cascade of becoming. It is only by being more conscious of this almost compulsory unfolding that we begin to comprehend the dynamic nature of reality.

The Hindrances

The Buddha described other frameworks by which we can "come and see." The following passages from the early discourses illustrate ways to connect with inner experience in order to gain familiarity with the living processes of mind and heart. For example, the five hindrances: overcoming these clears the way to deeper concentration and thereby conduces to the arising of insight.

> "Here, there being sensual desire in him, a bhikkhu understands: 'There is sensual desire in me'; or there being no sensual desire in him, he understands: 'There is no sensual desire in me'; and he also understands how there comes to be the arising of unarisen sensual desire, and how there comes to be the abandoning of arisen sensual desire, and how there comes to be the future non-arising of abandoned sensual desire.
>
> "There being ill will in him ... There being sloth and torpor in him ... There being restlessness and remorse in him ... There being doubt in him, a bhikkhu understands: 'There is doubt in me'; or there being no doubt in him, he understands: 'There is no doubt in me'; and he understands how there comes to be the arising of unarisen doubt, and how there comes to be the

abandoning of arisen doubt, and how there comes to be the future non-arising of abandoned doubt."[9]

In following the instructions of the Buddha, you learn in no uncertain terms where to inspect within the mind, how to place the attention. You grow more accountable to yourself, clearly differentiating the path to happiness from what leads to entanglement. Having settled the mind more firmly in introspection, practicing dexterity by recognizing common varieties of distraction, you are now ready to investigate consciousness itself.

The Fetters

The consciousness that arises at each sense door can be experienced as having both cause and effect, allure and drawback. Upon further contemplation, you will no longer be willing to settle for the trap of consciousness arising unawares. These next instructions describe the fetters, possible pitfalls, ways in which the heart and mind can be led astray.

> "Here a bhikkhu understands the eye, he understands forms, and he understands the fetter that arises dependent on both; and he also understands how there comes to be the arising of the unarisen fetter, and how there comes to be the abandoning of the arisen fetter, and how there comes to be the future non-arising of the abandoned fetter.
>
> "He understands the ear, he understands sounds . . . He understands the nose, he understands odours . . . He understands the tongue, he understands flavours . . . He understands the body, he understands tangibles . . . He understands the mind, he understands mind objects, and he understands the fetter that arises dependent on both; and he also understands how there comes to be the arising of the unarisen fetter, and how there comes to be the abandoning of the arisen fetter, and how there comes to be the future non-arising of the abandoned fetter."[10]

The Seven Enlightenment Factors

Guarding the doors of the senses and mind, protecting the field of aware-ness—now is the time to cultivate factors that foster the arising of insight wisdom. Please continue to follow the guidance of the Buddha while contemplating these suttas internally. The proper balance of these seven factors of enlightenment, when tended to perfection, will give rise quite naturally to awakening.

> "Here, there being the mindfulness enlightenment factor in him, a bhikkhu understands: 'There is the mindfulness enlightenment factor in me'; or there being no mindfulness enlightenment factor in him, he understands: 'There is no mindfulness enlightenment factor in me'; and he also under-stands how there comes to be the arising of the unarisen mind-fulness enlightenment factor, and how the arisen mindfulness enlightenment factor comes to fulfillment by development.
>
> "There being the investigation-of-states enlightenment factor in him . . . There being the energy enlightenment fac-tor in him . . . There being the rapture enlightenment factor in him . . . There being the tranquility enlightenment factor in him . . . There being the concentration enlightenment factor in him . . . There being the equanimity enlightenment factor in him, a bhikkhu understands: 'There is the equanimity enlight-enment factor in me'; or there being no equanimity enlighten-ment factor in him, he understands: 'There is no equanimity enlightenment factor in me'; and he also understands how there comes to be the arising of the unarisen equanimity enlightenment factor, and how the arisen equanimity enlight-enment factor comes to fulfillment by development."[11]

These are the very best ways to make good on the Buddha's invitation.

CHAPTER 2

Immediately Present Moments

BY NOW it is clear that suttas are not just pretty verses; they are pithy, step-by-step instructions of utmost clarity to be practiced here and now. One of the most famous utterances by Gotama Buddha was a single word: *ehipassiko*. It might be all that is needed to invite profound awakening to the way things are, to Dhamma. We can see for ourselves that this deceptively potent utterance is not an object to be grasped as an end in itself; rather, it points in a direction worthy of our attention.

When the mind is wondering or wandering about, we must "come and see" how quickly things are happening inside ourselves. Thoughts, phrases, sentences, discussions, sounds, feelings, sights, smells, touches, contacts; fantasies, daydreaming, vibrations; the lifelong beating of the heart, the unceasing expansion and contraction of the lungs; the flickering of light in the eyes; and many more activities are happening—all simultaneously. When we try to deal with even one of these occurrences, we find that many other marvelous tangles are already arising. They all appear and disappear. In the *Mahakaccanabhaddekaratta Sutta*, the monk Maha Kaccana recommends paying attention to "each presently arisen state." This means exactly whatever is going on right now. Then in the next moment. Now. When we pay attention to what is, without verbalizing or conceptualizing, all we notice is rising and falling. There are only states and objects coming into being and fading out of being.

From the *Bhaddekaratta Sutta*:

"Let not a person revive the past
Or on the future build his hopes;
For the past has been left behind
And the future has not been reached.
Instead with insight let him see
Each presently arisen state;
Let him know that and be sure of it,
Invincibly, unshakably.
Today the effort must be made;
Tomorrow Death may come, who knows?
No bargain with Mortality
Can keep him and his hordes away.
But one who dwells thus ardently,
Relentlessly, by day, by night—
It is he, the Peaceful Sage has said,
Who has had a single excellent night."[12]

Nobody can cause someone else to experience impermanence. You can only see it happening within yourself. As Maha Kaccana emphasizes, now is the only time we have in which to participate in this investigation. Our body, our excellent opportunity, only lasts for so long.

THREE MARKS OF EXISTENCE

The seeming reality to which you have direct inner access in meditation is ever-changing, and this has never been otherwise. This impermanence is one of the three marks of existence, which are said to hold true for all beings and for all existence.

1. All conditioned things are impermanent (*anicca*).
2. All conditioned things are unsatisfactory (*dukkha*).
3. All phenomena are without a separate self (*anatta*).

We observe changes in other people and other things, but often not within ourselves, unless we look within on purpose. Our bodies, feelings, perceptions, thoughts, and consciousnesses seem to us to be the same most of the time. Even if such things are obvious from the outside, it would sound funny to say to someone, "Hey, you are always changing." In order for the continuous unfolding of change to have a liberating effect, it must be known deeply and personally. It cannot be taught or memorized. The Dhamma is known when our inner seeing faculty turns to look at our deepest constellations of self without preconception.

BHANTE, WHAT HAPPENED?

Sometimes people who have not seen me for twenty years are surprised when they encounter me these days. They ask me, "Bhante, what happened?"

"Nothing special."

"I mean, you are changed," they say.

I do not turn around and ask them, "Do you think you have not changed?"

They see me grown old with wrinkles on my face and gray hair. My cheeks have sunk in. Everything in me shows the signs of old age. I can see their sunken cheeks, too, their gray hair and wrinkled skin. We can see what happens to friends and acquaintances, yet we do not notice what has happened to ourselves. This is a memo included with the invitation to "come and see."

When we do not see the marks of old age in our own bodies, we may look down upon others who have wizened like ourselves. Feeling young is pleasant if we notice it at all. At the same time, deep down, we experience all manner of aging: forgetting names, losing our appetite and ability to smell, decreased sensitivity in our fingertips, trouble sleeping, getting up to use the restroom more often in the night, as well as slowing mobility. These are only some of the common announcements by the body that it is getting old.

Accepting old age is an indication of a healthy mind. Once we do so, we are not irritated when we cannot function with the same agility, flexibility, and speed. Rejecting old age can lead us to lose our temper quickly if things do not work out as smoothly as when we were young. Aging is a built-in reminder. Pushing away what already has come into being is a frustrating and misguided strategy in the search for happiness.

Impermanence, suffering, and selflessness exist whether or not buddhas come into existence. Just look. Everything ages. Everything is changing. The principle of conditionality also exists whether or not any buddha comes into existence. Things and patterns of things depend upon other patterns and things. Vanishing and coming into being do not happen spontaneously, without processes having been already set in motion. If you look around you will see this too. The Buddha summarized dependent origination like this:

> This being, this comes to be.
> With the arising of this, this arises.
> This not being, this does not come to be.
> With the cessation of this, this ceases.[13]

The Buddha accepted the invitation to enter into this Dhamma. He followed the path of Dhamma and recognized a profound contingency in himself and in all things. Tracing each fundamental conditionality to its source, the Buddha saw the end of the repetitious cycle of birth and death.

The occasion to "come and see" welcomes all seekers to investigate the nature of phenomena (*dhammas*). The Buddha was shrewd in his experimentation. He described very carefully where and how to study the elements, their attributes, and their relationships with respect to cause and effect. He instructed those who aspired to liberation of mind that they should see impermanence, unsatisfactoriness, and selflessness for themselves.

Such research is impersonal because ceaseless change is happening in any body, any heap of elements or assembly of notions, all the time, regardless of ideology, opinion, creed, color, or gender. It is an invitation to come home, so to speak—to come home to our true selves and see what is there in this very being. In fact, every sutta delivered by the Buddha refers us back to ourselves, reminding us of our potential for an ancestral sort of homecoming—namely, that when we keep the mind in its proper range or skillful domain, as described in the basic teachings on the four foundations of mindfulness, we experience release; we see that our true home extends far beyond traditional constraints in time and space. Though the home we eventually find is all-pervasive, we access this resort via a particular turning of the heart and mind. We arrive home by crossing what the Buddha called the flood, without pushing or standing still.[14]

You find you within yourself, the Buddha urged. You cannot find yourself somewhere remote or entirely outside of yourself. He warned us not to leave this inner home unguarded. An unguarded home, the doors of the senses flung wide open, might be vulnerable to thieves or other disasters, hijacking mindfulness, robbing us of the chance for liberating insight. We need to be vigilant, the Buddha advised, and return home to safeguard what is there.

Quite literally, our home is the personal body and mind. There, everything we need to know to make us peaceful and happy, or to make us miserable and cause us to suffer, is happening all the time. *The Great Discourse on Mindfulness* repeats this message twenty-one times. The body, feelings, mental states, and related phenomena are opportunities for us to develop our understanding of impermanence, unsatisfactoriness, and no-self. Since both materiality and mentality are constantly changing right here, we can be mindful of their fluctuations. We do this by observing them with awareness, in awareness, as they transform and move.

THE QUAIL AND THE HAWK

The following parable teaches us that if we spend all of our time entertaining the senses without paying attention to the fluctuations taking place in our bodies and minds, we can be carried away by greed, hatred,

and delusion. These are the armies of Mara, the Buddhist personification of temptation, who offers sensual gratification and leads us by the
yoke of our likes and dislikes away from true freedom. Mara pretends to
help, enabling the chasing of petty wishes that never lead to happiness.
The Buddha told this little story to stress how important it is to stay in
our own domain while investigating Dhamma. The moment we leave our
domain and wander away we will be caught by Mara—our own mental
defilements.

> "Bhikkhus, once in the past a hawk suddenly swooped down
> and seized a quail. Then, while the quail was being carried off
> by the hawk, he lamented: 'We were so unlucky, of so little
> merit! We strayed out of our own resort into the domain of
> others. If we had stayed in our own resort today, in our own
> ancestral domain, this hawk wouldn't have stood a chance
> against me in a fight.' —'But what is your own resort, quail,
> what is your own ancestral domain?' – 'The freshly plowed
> field covered with clods of soil.'
>
> "Then the hawk, confident of her own strength, not boast-
> ing of her own strength, released the quail, saying, 'Go now,
> quail, but even there you won't escape me.'
>
> "Then, bhikkhus, the quail went to a freshly plowed field
> covered with clods of soil. Having climbed up on a large clod,
> he stood there and addressed the hawk: 'Come get me now,
> hawk! Come get me now!'
>
> "Then the hawk, confident of her own strength, not boast-
> ing of her own strength, folded up her wings and swooped
> down on the quail. But when the quail knew, 'That hawk has
> come close,' he slipped inside the clod, and the hawk shattered
> her breast right on the spot. So it is, bhikkhus, when one strays
> outside one's own resort into the domain of others.
>
> "Therefore, bhikkhus, do not stray outside your own resort

into the domain of others. Māra will gain access to those who stray outside their own resort into the domain of others; Māra will get a hold on them.

"And what is not a bhikkhu's own resort but the domain of others? It is the five cords of sensual pleasure. What five? Forms cognizable by the eye that are desirable, lovely, agreeable, pleasing, sensually enticing, tantalizing. Sounds cognizable by the ear . . . Odours cognizable by the nose . . . Tastes cognizable by the tongue . . . Tactile objects cognizable by the body that are desirable, lovely, agreeable, pleasing, sensually enticing, tantalizing. These are the five cords of sensual pleasure. This is what is not a bhikkhu's own resort but the domain of others.

"Move in your own resort, bhikkhus, in your own ancestral domain. Māra will not gain access to those who move in their own resort, in their own ancestral domain; Māra will not get a hold on them.

"And what is a bhikkhu's resort, his own ancestral domain? It is the four establishments of mindfulness. What four? Here, bhikkhus, a bhikkhu dwells contemplating the body in the body, ardent, clearly comprehending, mindful, having removed covetousness and displeasure in regard to the world. He dwells contemplating feelings in feelings . . . mind in mind . . . phenomena in phenomena, ardent, clearly comprehending, mindful, having removed covetousness and displeasure in regard to the world. This is a bhikkhu's resort, his own ancestral domain."[15]

In this parable the hawk represents Mara—greed, hatred, delusion, imaginations, fantasies and daydreams, planning for the future, pondering the past. All these things threaten our mindfulness and clear comprehension, which are represented by the quail. The Buddha is saying in this story that we must "come and see" our ancestral domain, return to our true home, just as the quail did. There we cannot be harmed by the attack of Mara.

What is happening now should be noted right away, without any delay. This means you should notice right this instant whatever is occurring in this very moment, neither before nor after. You will not find it in the next moment. Breath should be noticed as it comes in and goes out, not one single moment before or single moment after. Along with the breath, notice contact, feeling, perception, thought, attention, and consciousness—all of them arise and move on with the breath.

Merely See, Merely Hear, Merely Sense

The most direct teaching of "come and see" is given by the Buddha to Bahiya of the Bark Cloth.

> "Here, Bāhiya, you should train yourself thus: 'In the seen will be merely what is seen; in the heard will be merely what is heard; in the sensed will be merely what is sensed; in the cognized will be merely what is cognized.' In this way you should train yourself, Bāhiya.
>
> "When, Bāhiya, for you, 'In the seen is merely what is seen; in the heard is merely what is heard; in the sensed is merely what is sensed; in the cognized is merely what is cognized,' then, Bāhiya, you will not be 'with that.' When, Bāhiya, you are not 'with that,' then, Bāhiya, you will not be 'in that.' When, Bāhiya, you are not 'in that,' then, Bāhiya, you will be neither here nor beyond nor in between the two. Just this is the end of suffering."[16]

Bahiya was praised by the Buddha for following this guidance internally in his own mind and heart. In order for you to practice similarly, "what is seen; what is heard; what is cognized" should be recognized lightly in awareness as "merely seeing; merely hearing; merely sensing." Simply be aware in the moment of seeing, hearing, and sensing. And of the knowing.

Even with this brief instruction the Buddha points to how quickly sight, sound, sense, and mental cognition are subject to change. Luckily, in this story Bahiya of the Bark Cloth had developed his mindfulness such that he immediately grasped the meaning of the short discourse. Since interactions of seeing, hearing, sensing, and cognizing appear and disappear so swiftly, there is no time to put your "I" into the fleeting moments. When you perceive the sheer speed of change clearly, you also know intuitively that there is no time to dwell in any single happening. You do not invent a particular "experience" here and some "experience" out there; there is just happening. It also becomes obvious that lasting satisfaction cannot be found in any temporary stream of sense consciousness.

"Merely what is seen" does not even refer to objects that you have seen. It means only the fleeting moment of consciousness called "seeing" as it takes birth and dissolves again. It is neither subject nor object but rather the attention that is flowing dependent upon both. Similarly "merely what is heard" means the fleeting moment of hearing, "merely what is sensed" means the fleeting moment of sensing, and "merely what is cognized" means the fleeting moment of cognizing. You will know that you have fully scrutinized these rapid processes of seeing, hearing, sensing, and cognizing as they arise and change when you can no longer invest "I" or "my" or "mine" in any of these events. With this degree of clarity, you are freed from being bound up with sensory or mental experience. You will also know that the mind is not the same as those fleeting moments of consciousness.

Holding tightly to any perceiver, any object perceived, even any view, is stressful and not the way to freedom. In the very same way that you relax the muscles in your body for good health, you can relax the field of your mind. This verse from the *Suttanipata* reminds us that any point of view is still just a view:

"Behold the world together with its devas
conceiving a self in what is non-self.
Settled upon name-and-form,
they conceive: 'This is true.'

"In whatever way they conceive it,
it turns out otherwise.
That indeed is its falsity,
for the transient is of a false nature.

"Nibbana is of a non-false nature:
that the noble ones know as truth.
Through the breakthrough to truth,
hunger-less, they are fully quenched."[17]

While you are thinking, "I see" or "my vision" or "seeing is mine," the mere act of seeing is already gone, disappeared. This happens very quickly, in a split second. It is the nature of all conditioned things. They are fleeing any scene you create. This sometimes is called "moment-by-moment awareness" or "moment-by-moment mindfulness." You might incline your attention toward hearing, but in the instant of any further mental events, you find the same reality. So quickly. Already gone. There is no immovable mover to say "I." Mere action takes place. The apparent doer is only an ownerless grouping of processes. You might have heard of acquired self, mind-made self, formless self, gross acquired self. This is how all manner of self-notions evaporate.

 *Not Led Astray*

Sensual pleasures are your first army;
the second is called "discontent."
Hunger and thirst are the third;
the fourth is called "craving."

The fifth is dullness and drowsiness;
the sixth is called "cowardice."
Doubt is your seventh;
your eighth, denigration and pride.

Gain, praise, honor,
and wrongly obtained fame [is ninth];
[the tenth is when] one extols oneself
and looks down at others.

This is your army, Namuci,[18]
the squadron of the Dark One.
A weakling does not conquer it,
but having conquered it, one gains bliss.[19]

AT FIRST GLANCE, Mara might seem well supported by a cast of characters who uphold his antics. Mara's armies, however, are not permanent entities. They too appear and disappear. We can see them happening in us all the time. Mara's authority actually lies in the personal power of those who unconsciously give their own power over to his unexamined forces. Continuous mindfulness is the key to release from his dominion.

When sensual pleasures arise, we pay wise attention (*yoniso manasi-kara*) and immediately see the rising and falling of our breath, the rising and falling of feeling, perception, thoughts, attention, and consciousness. We must be well established in recognizing the rising and falling of these mental collections. As our awareness of the rising and falling of mental events grows stronger, we might even become interested in seeing the rising and falling of states of mind, also called *concomitants*. Interest in these building blocks of reality eventually attracts our attention more than Mara does, and we naturally lose interest in his armies. By withdrawing our attention, we disempower his threat. Seeing everything rising and falling is the secret; that is how the Buddha vanquished all the ten armies of Mara. There is no other magic in their defeat.

PERCEPTION OF IMPERMANENCE

The four stanzas above represent Mara's armies in a way that can be condensed into a triad, the basic perturbations in any heart that might otherwise be tranquil and clear. What are called the *three unwholesome roots* can be referred to broadly as greed (from sensual lust to mundane wanting), hatred (from outright rage to minor irritations), and ignorance (from gross delusion to plain not knowing). All three arise from the assumption that "I am," that one is a discrete, independently existing, separate, and unchanging entity. The source of unhappiness lies in this subtle type of ignorance. The Buddha tells us that the very perception of impermanence will dislodge that confusion, facilitating the falling away of all structures in the mind that depend upon the three unwholesome roots. "Come and see" invites investigation into whether "I am" is a valid assertion. While intellect alone might lead to dry philosophical analysis, remember that you can enjoy a more successful inquiry with the calm and joyful mind of concentration (*sukhino cittam samadhiyati*).

"Bhikkhus, when the perception of impermanence is developed and cultivated, it eliminates all sensual lust, it eliminates all lust for existence, it eliminates all ignorance, it uproots all conceit 'I am.'

"Just as, bhikkhus, in the autumn a ploughman ploughing with a great ploughshare cuts through all the rootlets as he ploughs, so too, when the perception of impermanence is developed and cultivated, it eliminates all sensual lust . . . it uproots all conceit 'I am.'

"Just as, bhikkhus, a rush-cutter would cut down a rush, grab it by the top, and shake it down and shake it out and thump it about, so too, when the perception of impermanence is developed and cultivated, it eliminates all sensual lust . . . it uproots all conceit 'I am.'

"Just as, bhikkhus, when the stalk of a bunch of mangoes has been cut, all the mangoes attached to the stalk follow along with it, so too, when the perception of impermanence is developed . . . it uproots all conceit 'I am.'

"Just as, bhikkhus, all the rafters of a house with a peaked roof lead to the roof peak, slope toward the roof peak, and converge upon the roof peak, and the roof peak is declared to be their chief, so too, when the perception of impermanence is developed . . . it uproots all conceit 'I am.'

"Just as, bhikkhus, among fragrant roots, black orris is declared to be their chief, so too, when the perception of impermanence is developed . . . it uproots all conceit 'I am.'

"Just as, bhikkhus, among fragrant heartwoods, red sandalwood is declared to be their chief, so too, when the perception of impermanence is developed . . . it uproots all conceit 'I am.'

"Just as, bhikkhus, among fragrant flowers, jasmine is declared to be their chief, so too, when the perception of impermanence is developed . . . it uproots all conceit 'I am.'

"Just as, bhikkhus, all petty princes are the vassals of a wheel-turning monarch, and the wheel-turning monarch is declared to be their chief, so too, when the perception of impermanence is developed . . . it uproots all conceit 'I am.'

"Just as, bhikkhus, the radiance of all the stars does not amount to a sixteenth part of the radiance of the moon, and the radiance of the moon is declared to be their chief, so too, when the perception of impermanence is developed . . . it uproots all conceit 'I am.'

"Just as, bhikkhus, in the autumn, when the sky is clear and cloudless, the sun, ascending in the sky, dispels all darkness from space as it shines and beams and radiates, so too, when the perception of impermanence is developed and cultivated, it eliminates all sensual lust, it eliminates all lust for existence, it eliminates all ignorance, it uproots all conceit 'I am.'

"And how, bhikkhus, is the perception of impermanence developed and cultivated so that it eliminates all sensual lust, eliminates all lust for existence, eliminates all ignorance, and uproots all conceit 'I am?' 'Such is form, such its origin, such its passing away; such is feeling . . . such is perception . . . such are volitional formations . . . such is consciousness, such its origin, such its passing away.' That is how the perception of impermanence is developed and cultivated so that it eliminates all sensual lust, eliminates all lust for existence, eliminates all ignorance, and uproots all conceit 'I am.'[20]

Beautiful imagery reminds us that our diligent investigation must be paired with inspiration, even awe, to best support our emerging direct knowing of impermanence. It is best to balance a sense of urgent examination with easy curiosity. Then discern each immediate sensory perception of form, the single subsequent moment of pleasant or unpleasant or neither, the arising of memory and perception based upon that flash of feeling, and the cascade of proliferating thought formations along with their associated volitions. Every sense phenomenon, every thought formation, should be noticed. This entire process, when seen and understood, is nothing short of miraculous. With practice you can experience directly that open sky with the bright and peaceful moon. You can even know the sun.

Making the Best Use of Now

Dhamma, the truth, lives in us and with us. If we do not pay attention to it, if we wander away from our ancestral domain, we are unaware of how it exists in us. The truth that we experience all the time, whether we notice it or not, is Dhamma—wholesome, unwholesome, neutral, or imperturbable. This Dhamma is constantly inviting us, saying, "Look at me, look at me. Do not ignore me. If you ignore me, you will be in trouble. If you want to be free from trouble, pay attention to me and take care of me." And how to take care of Dhamma? We should not forget it. We should not forget that we are moving on with a one-way ticket. Every moment we are moving on toward the inevitable—old age, sickness, and death. Therefore, we must make the best use of this very precious moment. We must not feel sorry later, saying, "I wish I had started this practice twenty, thirty years earlier."

We are each a profound example of impermanence, alive and in motion. The treasure of a human body is a great gift and an opportunity. By taking care, with mindfulness, of this living, breathing process, we perceive Dhamma more and more deeply; it is teaching us, and we can realize our full potential. Otherwise, there might not be peace now or when we die.

"Come and see" also means that we should use requisites, those things we need in order to continue living in this physical body, mindfully.

Monks generally receive four such necessities: clothing, food, shelter, and medicines. As human animals, we know that we are always in relationship with the sources of our requisites. Sometimes the supplier of our basic needs is nearby, and it is obvious how such a thing came into our lives. Other times the food was grown and prepared elsewhere, the fabric woven far away, the medicine made by fellow beings unseen, the shelter built in community. We can recollect the loveliness of the chance to live and feel and breathe because we have these supports for the continued existence of the body. If we use requisites mindfully, we are living a noble and pure life, which can inspire others to do the same. This kind of being is called "blameless." We can inspire those around us to feel safe and happy. This encourages the spread of *metta*, or loving-friendliness. So "come and see" is a friendly challenge, an invitation to profound Dhamma imbued with simple kindness, too.

CHAPTER 4

Pointing to Impermanence

SEEING IMPERMANENCE as reality rather than just a nice idea has profound implications. It is by way of impermanence that the Buddha proved the absence of an inherently separate self. Let us consider how he nudged the minds of his five ascetic friends toward enlightenment.

It is said that a buddha can know which words or activities will direct the mindstream of a person most effectively toward enlightenment. Despite this ability to discern the capacities of those whom he met, the Buddha was reluctant to teach the first few folks he encountered after his awakening. In fact, he abstained from divulging his attainment of instructional powers until he received a very convincing request to teach and reconnected with the famous group of five former companions. The Buddha then distilled his realization into functional teaching points and delivered his first formal discourses. He chose different words and similes for different types of hearers, but in one way or another, they all pointed to impermanence.

The first sermon the Buddha gave after his awakening was called the *Dhammacakkappavattana Sutta, The Discourse on Turning the Wheel of Dhamma.*[21] In the radiant presence of the liberated heart of their former peer, resistance among the five ascetics melted away. Upon hearing that there is a middle way between austerity and indulgence, they could not disagree and grew receptive. When the Buddha pointed out the pain inherent in fixation on anything, the grip of their minds loosened. At that moment, through hearing and contemplating the Buddha's words, only the ascetic Kondanna saw that what is subject to arising is also subject to passing away. This is how Kondanna's mind and heart inclined irrevocably toward the perception of impermanence. This is how the first of the five attained stream entry, the first stage of enlightenment.

The next day the Buddha asked all five of his old friends, the group of ascetics, a series of questions during his second formal discourse, the *Anattalakkhana Sutta, The Discourse on the Characteristic of No Self*:

> "What do you think, bhikkhus? Is form permanent or impermanent? . . . Is feeling permanent or impermanent? . . . Is perception permanent or impermanent? . . . Are mental formations permanent or impermanent? . . . Is consciousness permanent or impermanent?"
>
> "Impermanent, venerable sir."
>
> "Is that which is impermanent unsatisfactory or satisfactory?"
>
> "Unsatisfactory, venerable sir."
>
> "Is it correct to consider that which is impermanent, unsatisfactory, and of the nature to change as 'this is mine, this I am, this is my self?'"
>
> "No, venerable sir."
>
> "Therefore, bhikkhus, whatever form . . . feeling . . . perception . . . mental formations . . . consciousness, whether past, future, or present, internal or external, gross or subtle, low or high, far or near, all forms . . . feelings . . . perceptions . . . mental formations . . . consciousness are not mine, I am not them, nor are they my self. Thus it should be correctly seen with wisdom as it is.
>
> "Perceiving thus, bhikkhus, the learned and noble disciple becomes disenchanted with form, feeling, perception, mental formations, and consciousness. And that disciple, through this disenchantment, becomes dispassionate, and by the absence of

passion, free, and when free, aware of that freedom, aware that rebirth is exhausted, that the holy life has been lived, that there is nothing more to do."

Thus spoke the Sublime One. Delighted, the group of five bhikkhus rejoiced in what the Sublime One had said. While this exposition was being delivered, without attachment, the group of five bhikkhus became free from the defilements. Then there were six arahants in the world.[22]

What had once seemed so convincingly solid, they now understood to be merely an assemblage of other impermanent parts. What once compelled their minds so strongly, they now perceived as contingencies of passing thoughts. In comprehending transience, the remaining four ascetics deeply realized the drawbacks of clinging to anything in the world. They lost their enchantment with the world but found peace.

IMPERMANENCE OF THE AGGREGATES AND SENSES

When invited to look at the impermanence of their own aggregates,[23] all five ascetics gained liberation through directed self-inquiry. In the Buddha's time this approach worked for a variety of people, guiding both men and women toward the goal of awakening. The *Nandakovada Sutta* echoes the same style of question and response. In this case Venerable Nandaka posed questions to a large group of bhikkhunis, or female monastics, asking them whether the internal six senses, their respective external objects, the consciousnesses that seemingly arose from and between them, or even the related contact and feelings were permanent or impermanent:

> "Sisters, what do you think? Is the eye permanent or impermanent?"—"Impermanent, venerable sir."—"Is what is impermanent suffering or happiness?"—"Suffering, venerable sir."—

"Is what is impermanent, suffering, and subject to change fit to be regarded thus: 'This is mine, this I am, this is my self?'"—"No, venerable sir."[24]

In this story Venerable Nandaka repeated the same series of questions regarding the remaining senses, such as hearing and so forth, all the way up to the mind, as well as in relation to their respective sensory objects, consciousness, contacts, and feelings arising from contact. To the example of each sense door, the bhikkhunis' response was the same: They could find not a single sense phenomenon, no sight, sound, smell, taste, or touch; neither emotion nor feeling; not even a thought that would last long enough to be considered a self. Then Venerable Nandaka dismissed them, asking them to go to the Buddha to clarify any remaining doubts they might have.

This particular teaching proved so effective that the Buddha advised Venerable Nandaka to repeat the talk again the following day. It is said that every single one of those bhikkunis was satisfied with the instruction and even the least of them gained entry to the stream of enlightenment. They overcame their doubts by seeing through the deception of the senses: neither sense organ, nor sense object, nor the acts of sensing or feeling, is self. Each bhikkhuni realized herself to be fleeting points of attention, woven together anew in each instant by the mind. This is the power of impermanence when seen as it really is.

 *Root Cause*

THE BUDDHA, despite his profound realization, was not entirely immune to common maladies. He was said to have back pain, and we know he got food poisoning. We can also assume that there were mosquitos when he lived in India just like there are today. It feels so good to scratch their itchy bites, but we all know what happens after a good scratch; the skin feels even more itchy. There are stories of people trying not to itch and scratch and swat at insects, who then end up swatting at one another instead.

Advertisers and substance abusers know this well; when we are not fully conscious of what bugs us, we humans can do illogical things. If we need a nap, we might drink a stimulating drink, which actually prevents rest. Someone susceptible to alcohol might want to be accepted and feel at ease in a group but then have a drink and end up doing stupid things instead. You might purchase some unnecessary object and feel not quite right about it. You go shopping again to get a slightly different one. Then you have two objects that you never needed in the first place.

There is an itch that can arise in the mind, and mindfulness allows us to see its root cause without adding absurdity. We might not be able to stop all physical discomfort, but we can pay attention to irritation when it arises and keep the agitation from getting the better of us.

Buy One, Get One Free

As human beings, we experience both pleasure and pain through our form (body), feelings, perceptions, formations, and consciousness. For the most part we prefer pleasure to pain. We enjoy having a healthy body, pleasant feelings, pleasant perceptions, good thoughts, and a clarifying of consciousness.

We enjoy pleasure in the present and hope to have more of it in the future. We take certain precautions to try to avoid pain now and in the future. We buy health insurance to help pay our medical bills; we buy insurance for our cars, our houses, and even for our lives. We hope all those policies will pay for physical injuries and property loss. Some of us save money for our funeral expenses.

But of course, pleasure can quickly change into pain. This is the intrinsic nature of everything. Along with pleasure comes pain, which we do not invite; even as we are enjoying pleasure, pain somehow sneaks in. The inevitable result is unhappiness. Along with our happiness comes suffering.

This is the ultimate "buy one, get one free" offer. If you experience pleasure and happiness, you will inevitably experience pain and suffering as well. They are inseparable, parts of the same package. You must buy the entire package. That is the deal.

Often people say, "I'm exhausted from my vacation. I need another vacation to recover from my vacation." So true! You overwork in your job in order to earn some time to have a good vacation. Then during your vacation you overwork at relaxing and having fun. Maybe you try harder to get the most out of all the extra work you did saving up. With the pleasure comes pain. As we develop mindfulness we become aware of this self-operating system of pleasure and pain. We learn to say, "Let come what comes" and begin to accept the "buy one, get one free" deal.

Getting What One Wants Is Suffering

The Buddha advised his followers:

> Bhikkhus, one who seeks delight in form seeks delight in suffering. One who seeks delight in suffering, I say, is not freed from

suffering. One who seeks delight in feeling... in perception ... in volitional formations... in consciousness seeks delight in suffering. One who seeks delight in suffering, I say, is not freed from suffering. One who does not seek delight in form ... in consciousness does not seek delight in suffering. One who does not seek delight in suffering, I say, is freed from suffering.[25]

In fact, any person who enjoys sensual pleasures also "enjoys" suffering. They do not know that they are enjoying suffering because they do not understand how suffering lurks under the excitement of pleasure. Suppose, for example, that someone is eating a very delicious piece of cake that happens to be full of poison. It may taste delicious, but they do not know that they are killing themself by eating this poisoned cake. They enjoy the taste. Similarly, the Buddha said that one who enjoys pleasure enjoys suffering:

> It is this craving that leads to renewed existence, accompanied by delight and lust, seeking delight here and there; that is, craving for sensual pleasures, craving for existence, craving for extermination. This is called the root of misery.[26]

GETTING WHAT ONE DOES NOT WANT IS SUFFERING

One of the most familiar forms of suffering is not getting what we want, not having our wishes fulfilled. The flip side of that coin is getting what we do not want. That, too, brings suffering. Here are some examples:

Birth. Who wants to be born again? Perhaps no one. You may say, "One life is enough. I have gone through so much in this life. I don't want another life." That's an understandable wish. Perhaps it will come true, perhaps not. Who knows? We can make aspirations; we can optimize causes and conditions. But uncertainty remains; many of us feel we have no control over this whatsoever. So, it is possible you will be born again against your wishes. This is suffering.

Aging. Another common wish is not to grow old. We see how older people suffer, both physically and mentally. They can no longer eat everything they want to; they cannot move as quickly or as smoothly as they used to. They lose their independence, bit by bit. Who wants to grow old? Hardly anyone. So often we try to stop the natural progression of aging: We cover up our wrinkles, our gray hair, our blurry vision, broken teeth, and fading hearing. We pretend we are not getting older. But no matter how hard we pretend to be young, we are still experiencing the frustrations of aging. Ultimately we cannot stop this process. We do not want it to happen, but it does. We get what we do not want. This is suffering.

Sickness. No one enjoys being sick, so we have developed all kinds of preventive measures to try to keep ourselves in good health: exercise routines, healthy diets, pills, massages, oils, and lotions. All of these things are designed to prevent us from getting ill. Even so, we do eventually get sick. We might get better for a time, but there is no guarantee that we will not eventually fall sick again. None of these miracle cures can prevent illness forever. This is suffering.

Death. Modern medicine has plenty of surgeries, medications, and therapies that help us extend human life. But ultimately we are only postponing the inevitable. No one so far has found a way to stop death forever. Even though death is very much a part of life, we somehow wish it will never come to us. Yet it does. This is suffering.

Sorrow. Whenever we lose something we love—a job, a possession, a beloved person—we feel sorrow. This is a normal and natural response to the loss. But sorrow is an uncomfortable, unpleasant experience. We do not want it, and yet it comes to us in the wake of a loss. This is suffering.

Pain. Physical pain is a feature of having a physical body. Even enlightened people feel pain. As long as you have a brain and nervous system you will at some point feel pain. We generally do not enjoy it, but it comes. This is suffering.

Grief. Just as with sorrow, the unpleasant experience of grieving a loss is something we do not wish for. We see others grieving, and we hope it will not happen to us. But eventually it does. We will lose people or things we love, and the grieving takes its own course. This is suffering.

Despair. Feelings of despair and hopelessness are also unwelcome. We do not like experiencing those emotions, and yet they too arise against our wishes. This is suffering.

WHAT IS THE CAUSE OF DEATH?

All these forms of suffering that we inevitably experience, despite our not wanting them, are actually pointers to the root cause of death. When human beings and animals die, sometimes pathologists are called in to determine the cause of death, but the Buddha found one universally true cause of death: birth. He spoke of this to his personal attendant, Venerable Ananda:

> "It was said: 'With birth as condition there is aging and death.' How this is so, Ananda, should be understood in this way: If there were absolutely and utterly no birth of any kind anywhere—that is, of gods into the state of gods, of celestials into the state of celestials, of spirits, demons, human beings, quadrupeds, winged creatures, and reptiles, each into their own state—if there were no birth of beings of any sort into any state, then, in the complete absence of birth, with the cessation of birth, would aging and death be discerned?"
>
> "Certainly not, venerable sir."
>
> "Therefore, Ananda, this is the cause, source, origin, and condition for aging and death, namely, birth."[27]

When somebody passes away, a coroner may perform an autopsy and conclude that the person passed away due to heart failure, kidney failure, a stroke, or some other organ malfunction. A politician, on the other hand, may say that poverty caused the person's death, that they were unable to afford suitable food or medicine or could not get to a hospital, or that this person's death occurred for some other economic reason. A religious leader may say that the person's bad habits caused their death: perhaps the person was an alcoholic and developed liver cancer, or they were a chain smoker. But the Buddha's diagnosis is very simple and universally true; that is, the cause of anybody's death is birth.

From the moment we are born we are marching toward one inevitable destination. We are born with a one-way ticket. We cannot go back even one fraction of a second. A medical miracle may delay death, but eventually each and every human life ends in death.

CHAPTER 6

Dhamma Talks to Us

BEING WITHIN US, Dhamma "talks" to us all the time. We do not hear it; it is as if we are deaf. We do not see the Dhamma, either; it is as if we are blind. We ignore it. This is our ignorance. Wherever we go, Dhamma is there, but we do not necessarily notice it. Our attention is elsewhere. Despite the fact that we ignore it, Dhamma goes with us. Just as for fishes made of water, the stream in which they swim seems invisible; just as birds with hollow bones fly through an unseen sky, we cannot separate from Dhamma.

It is not something we can see with our eyes. Dhamma is an experience. Although we are actually awash with Dhamma all the time, our ignorance stops us from seeing it in our lives and our experience. We are blind to it, or we pay only superficial attention. And then, unfortunately, we become even more ignorant. When we are blinded by greed, hate, fear, and confusion, we cannot pay attention to the reality underneath those emotions. How often do we see only the injustice and unfairness of others but not our own bias and prejudice? We might even claim that we ourselves practice Dhamma while saying that another person is only pretending to practice Dhamma.

The Buddha, however, recognized the difference between those who truly practice Dhamma and those who do not. He said that there are beings who have "only a little dust in their eyes." When the Buddha started teaching Dhamma, those who had only this little bit of dust in their eyes began to feel a tingling. They brought attention to a new sensation and rubbed this prickling from the inside. In so doing they wiped the dust from their eyes—enabling them to see Dhamma. They began to view reality in a new and different way; they could see and understand the truth of things just as they are without anything added. That is what happened to Siddhattha Gotama himself, the man from the Sakya clan who sat down to meditate diligently under a tree and became the Buddha. When that dust in his eyes was wiped away, he saw the light of Dhamma. In fact, in his first sermon after attaining enlightenment, he said, "Light arose in me. Wisdom arose in me. Knowledge arose in me."[28] With that light, he stated that he saw Dhamma operating in ten thousand world systems.

It is important to know that Dhamma actually predates every buddha who has ever been born. Whether buddhas come into this world or not, this established Dhamma, the law of Dhamma, the natural law of the way things are, exists. The mission of all buddhas is to realize this natural order and to comprehend it in its entirety. Then they teach Dhamma, point it out, establish it, open it, analyze it, and make it known to the world.

What Is This Dhamma That Invites Us?

What is this Dhamma? Fundamentally it involves direct experience of the three marks of existence: impermanence (*anicca*), lack of a separate self (*anatta*), and suffering or unsatisfactoriness (*dukkha*). With personal perception of these qualities in a sustained manner, that suffering can point us to peace (*nibbana*). Once again, we are invited to "come and see."

The truth, whether or not we call it the "Truth" with a capital T, is present in our minds and bodies all the time; it constantly invites our attention. But we hardly ever stop and look at what is going on inside the mind and body. The actuality that we experience all the time is the Dhamma. Dhamma reminds us that we can learn from noticing the process instead of the things.

Dust Talks to Us

Imagine a nice, clean room. It has six doors. All the doors are open. Through those open doors, wind blows dust from outside into the room. You want to clean the room, so you sweep up the dust that has blown in. But the next day the dust is there again. After several days' sweeping, you decide to mop the room. You bring a bucket of water and a mop, and you clean the room. But lo and behold, the dust just keeps blowing in, day after day. So, one day you decide to pour a concrete floor in the room, hoping that may keep it clean. But of course it does not. More dust! Finally you decide to close all the doors, and that is what does the trick: at last, a clean room.

Similarly, you may observe wholesome precepts from time to time to purify your mind. But at unmindful moments you break one or more of your intended precepts, so you make a commitment to repeat your precepts and start over. Abstaining from unwholesome activities really can positively affect the content that arises in the mind. However, no matter how many times you start over, you tend to break your precepts. Old and dusty mental states can return. Then you decide to add another method of purifying your mind by practicing meditation. As you do, you gain concentration and reach deep states called *jhana*, during which your senses are temporarily closed to outside stimuli. Your mind becomes free of defilements, or clean—just as the room stayed clean when you finally closed the doors. However, as soon as you come out of the jhana state and your senses are exposed to sensory objects, you will find that mental defilements (or dust) rush back in. So long as there are still unresolved latent tendencies, called fetters and hindrances in this tradition, the heart and mind have not yet been cleaned in a lasting way. When hang-ups or patterns that generate the dust of human stress still lie dormant beneath any temporary state of peacefulness, your mind cannot be totally free of defilements. Only when such fetters are completely eliminated can the mind be free of all possibility of becoming defiled (or dusty) again.

BAMBOO TALKS TO US

Hindrances are like bamboo plants. Once one of our residents at Bhavana Society was getting ready to plant a bamboo sapling right beneath my bedroom window. "Don't plant it there," I said. "When it grows, it will block the view I enjoy every day."

"Don't worry!" the resident said. "This is not Asia. Bamboo will not grow that fast here."

He planted it right by my window—and within a year it was almost six feet tall. The next year, the "mother" plant produced a crop of young saplings that popped out of the ground all around it. Within three years my view was completely blocked by the bamboo grove flourishing outside my window. I called the person who planted the original plant and asked him to come and remove it. He dug it out, but six months later more bamboo shoots appeared. He returned with a bulldozer and thoroughly churned up the ground in that spot. A few months later: more shoots. It took a third round of excavation by another resident, using digging bar, hoe, and pickax to unearth every single bamboo root left in the ground.

Similarly, fetters and underlying tendencies are the groundwork for hindrances. As long as the fetters remain, familiar mental hindrances will continue to grow each time we come out of jhana meditation. Even a modicum of a tendency—one remaining bamboo shoot—can sprout a new thicket of hindrances. But when deep insight uproots all the fetters, or ties that bind our minds and hearts, then the hindrances will never arise again.

Here is a way to bring such insight into your own life: Maybe you get angry with someone. Your first impulse will probably be to focus on what that other person did to you, but instead try looking at your own mind. Ask yourself how much you suffer from your anger. Similarly, let us suppose you want something very badly, but you cannot have it, so greed arises in you. Instead of focusing on that thing you want so much, look within and see how much you are suffering because of your greed. Or maybe you are jealous or envious of someone's achievement or success. Look at your own mind and investigate how much suffering you are experiencing because of your envy or jealousy. When you see an arrogant person, you might get upset. Instead of concentrating on how arrogant he is, you can notice how you feel when you see such arrogance. Reflect on how other people might feel if you yourself displayed arrogance; they would probably feel the same as you are feeling in that moment. When the consequence of giving rise to such a state, namely the resultant unpleasant feeling, becomes absolutely clear, somehow the mind is no longer willing to generate that particular emotional quality. Whether or not this recognition of pain is conscious, the sensitive heart simply ceases to go there. This is the way to "come and see" the Dhamma within yourself.

We can also use "come and see" to explore positive states of mind and heart. If you witness someone doing something compassionate, for example, look into your own heart and ask yourself how much compassion you have. If compassion does not arise naturally, you can try doing something kind to help someone else and see if that arouses compassion. When you see someone full of joy, examine how much joy you have within yourself. If you do not feel joyful, try giving something to someone without expecting anything in return. Or let go of some little thing you like and see if that produces the joy of not worrying about little things. See how much you enjoy being relaxed rather than uptight and rigid. Joy tends to grow when we gain deeper concentration and insight, when we see truth as it actually is. Let the stream of that pure joy flow into a broad and powerful river rather than deceiving yourself with a stream of less true ideas. Protect your mind from invading greed, hatred, and delusion. No enemy can do as much harm to you as your own harmful thoughts. Just as a creeper vine strangles and kills the tree that supports the vine, harmful thoughts can destroy your peace and make your life miserable.

The Buddha warned us explicitly about this: "By oneself is evil done; by oneself is one defiled. By oneself is evil left undone; by oneself is one made pure. Purity and impurity depend on oneself; no one can purify another."[29] And he did not avoid the topic of personal responsibility, of cause and effect: "Just as rust arising from iron eats away the base from which it arises, even so, their own deeds lead transgressors to states of woe."[30] In these exhortations the Buddha still guides us today to look within and see how much misery we create in ourselves just with our own thoughts. Conversely, if we establish ourselves in a steady practice of mindfulness, we will create occasions for peace and happiness. This recognition is the exact aim of the invitation to "come and see."

SIXTY PLACES WHERE GREED ARISES

You can see Dhamma every fraction of a second if you pay attention to your mind and body. The Buddha asked us to see Dhamma with the body and senses (*dhammam kayena passati*).[31] We can also see Dhamma in the personality. You cannot see Dhamma in books or supermarkets. If we pay attention mindfully, we can see sixty places where the greed that causes suffering arises, and with mindful practice of Dhamma we can dissolve those same sixty greedy moments and liberate ourselves from suffering.

1. *Senses*: Craving arises in the pleasant and agreeable nature of the eyes, the ears, the nose, the tongue, the body, and the mind.
2. *Sensory objects*: Craving arises in the pleasant and agreeable nature of forms, sounds, odors, tastes, tactile objects, and mental phenomena.
3. *Consciousness*: Craving arises in the pleasant and agreeable nature of eye-consciousness, ear-consciousness, tongue-consciousness, nose-consciousness, body-consciousness, and mind-consciousness.
4. *Contacts*: Craving arises in the pleasant and agreeable nature of eye-contact, ear-contact, nose-contact, tongue-contact, body-contact, and mind-contact.
5. *Feelings*: Craving arises in the pleasant and agreeable nature of feeling born of eye-contact, ear-contact, nose-contact, tongue-contact, body-contact, and mind-contact.

6. *Perceptions*: Craving arises in the pleasant and agreeable nature of perception of forms, sounds, odors, tastes, tactile objects, and mental phenomena.

7. *Volitions*: Craving arises in the pleasant and agreeable nature of volition regarding forms, sounds, odors, tastes, tactile objects, and mental phenomena.

8. *Craving*: Craving arises in the pleasant and agreeable nature of craving for forms, sounds, odors, tastes, tactile objects, and mental phenomena.

9. *Thoughts*: Craving arises in the pleasant and agreeable nature of the thought of forms, sounds, odors, tastes, tactile objects, and mental phenomena.

10. *Examination*: Craving arises in the pleasant and agreeable nature of the examination of forms, sounds, odors, tastes, tactile objects, and mental phenomena.[32]

In these sixty places where craving arises and settles, we can actually see craving arising from craving itself; it perpetuates and multiplies itself. That is why the Buddha referred to this craving as "re-becoming" (*ponobhavika*) and "endowed with delight and clinging" (*nandiragasahagata*). It is the sort of delight that is distracting instead of liberating. "Delighting here and there" (*tatratatrabhinandini*), each time craving arises, suffering arises along with it. And to end suffering, the reverse is true. In the very same discourse, the Buddha showed that where craving arises, that is precisely where it should be eliminated. Doing this, you put an end to suffering.

SUFFERING TURNS INTO HAPPINESS

Both mindful and unmindful persons experience objects through their senses. Mindful persons, however, learn to use their experiences to arouse peace and happiness. They see reality just as it is and can delight in the fleeting experience at any sense door without the delusion that it will last, without the pain of wanting more or less of it. Unmindful persons let their senses bring suffering to them, for they do not see reality. The reality in all things is that they are impermanent. Seeing impermanence is a pleasure—if there are no strings attached.

One day the Buddha went to the demon Alavaka's mansion, but when he arrived there, Alavaka was missing. He had gone out following the passions of a demon. His wives were there, however, and they welcomed the Buddha inside. The Buddha sat down and began to teach them Dhamma. Meanwhile, the demon Alavaka came back to his mansion. Seeing the Buddha talking to his wives, he became upset and requested that the Buddha get out of his mansion. The Buddha went out. Then the demon asked the Buddha to return. The Buddha did so. For a second time, Alavaka told the Buddha to leave but then wanted his return. Finally, the demon ordered the Buddha for a third time to get out, but this time the Buddha challenged the demon. He said, "I will not go out." So, the demon posed several riddles for the Buddha. Although the questions were framed by the demon's rough character, the Buddha did not fall into hostility. Not ensnared by his own heart's response, he was able to turn each question around, emphasizing enjoyment without clinging in relation to sense pleasures, instead of in the ways of demons. Alavaka asked: "What is the tastiest of all the tastes?" The Buddha answered, "Truth indeed is the tastiest of all the tastes" (*saccam have sadhutaram rasanam*).[33] The demon was especially pleased with this reply.

You might think that the Buddha, in refusing to leave the demon's mansion, was discourteous in this episode. But the Buddha knew quite well that he had gone there for a very specific mission: to teach the demon Dhamma. When the Buddha finished answering each question that Alavaka had asked, the demon's heart was gladdened; he attained stream entry, the first level of enlightenment, and he stopped giving rise to mean thoughts, words, and deeds. Finally, he went from village to village and city to city teaching the truth of Dhamma.

"What is this truth?" you may ask. The answer is impermanence. Ordinary people who do not meditate, or those who meditate incorrectly, experience numerous things through their senses and suffer. Mindful meditators experience almost the same things that unmindful people do; the difference is that mindful persons see impermanence in everything, which is the truth. Seeing this truth, they are delighted.

> Fully knowing
> the arising and passing of the *khandhas*,[34]
> one attains joy and delight.
> For those who know, this is the Deathless.[35]

CHAPTER 7

Diminishing Returns

DIMINISHING RETURNS is a basic law of economics. There are certain things we wish to obtain, and sometimes we obtain them. Then as we enjoy a certain thing repeatedly, we gradually lose interest in it. For example, many people desire to find a life partner and spend a lot of time and energy looking for that special person. After a long search you find someone who seems to be a perfect match for you. You feel happy and assume that this relationship will last forever. Before too long, though, your partner starts changing—and so do you. Both your and your partner's feelings, perceptions, thoughts, attitudes, and interest in the other person are changing. Meanwhile, each of you might notice someone else enticing. You grow interested in that other person, and your partner is interested in someone else, too. Your relationship slowly starts cooling down. Very subtly—or maybe not so subtly—you begin to dislike your partner, even feeling irritated toward them. Irritation grows into anger and then contempt. You decide to separate, and then you are dealing with all the issues of dividing property and settling on custody arrangements for your children. You are living the law of diminishing returns.

Similarly, many people experience the law of diminishing returns when it comes to their children. The urge to have children starts out as a strong desire to be a parent. Once the desire becomes a reality, though, the parents sometimes struggle with all the responsibilities and difficulties of rearing children. On the one hand, they are happy to have a family;

on the other hand, it can cause them a great deal of pain. What was originally a joy can grow into a difficult task.

You wish for an ideal life. But you end up with an unhappy one. There is always friction between what you want and what you get.

Here is another example: You buy a very expensive car, something you have been dreaming of for a long time. The next day you go out for errands, park in front of a shop, and go inside to buy something. When you come back in ten minutes you see a long scratch along the side of your beautiful, new car. You do not know who did it, but you are furious with them. You love your brand-new, expensive car. But now there is frustration and anger—suffering—alongside the joy.

The suffering in this example is caused by your attachment to this car. When I say "attachment," I speak metaphorically. Of course, no person can attach to an inanimate object. The attachment is actually your thought, your wish to possess this car and identify it as belonging to you. But this wish is a dream because everything changes. We cannot possess anything, or anyone, in its present state because its state will change. As we change, the things we want to possess change. And as they change, we change. Change dominates our lives. Everything in the universe, and therefore our every relationship with everything, is changing every nanosecond.

The On-I-On

The moment we are born, greed and ignorance are also born, and they meet immediately. This pair—greed and ignorance—are in the mind. We never see them in flesh and blood, but we can feel their presence in our mind.

At their very first meeting, greed and ignorance recognize each other and fall in love. They have known each other from time immemorial, ever since they moved into *samsara* together.[36] Having met again here in this life, their sense of familiarity does not take long to grow into deep devotion to one other. They marry instantly without any dating, matchmaking, ceremony, or ritual. They do not have a religion, nor do they require one. As soon as they have married, ignorance makes greed pregnant.

Greed does not have to wait any time for this embryo to grow. Almost simultaneously with their marriage, she delivers her one and only baby, which they name "I." They know that they have a baby, but they never see their baby. They just mutter the word *I* with great adoration. Almost all of their thoughts and emotions arise in relation to I. Day and night, they protect their unseen newborn, sitting on either side of it. The father, ignorance, sits *on* one side, and the mother, greed, sits *on* the other side of I. And so I is sandwiched snugly between them. On-I-On, or Onion.

Occupying the center of attention between its two parents, this somehow-intangible child, I, tightens the bond between craving and ignorance.

This union of On-I-On is so deceptive that when you look, it seems to have some core to it. But though you peel away layer after layer of an onion looking for pith, while you might cry a lot, you never find much inside. The essence called *I* is imagined. Greed, on one side, and ignorance, on the other, create the illusion of I in the On-I-On, with constant opportunity for distraction either way you turn. The tantalizing image of some spicy, bulb-like root is mind made. Similarly, the "I" in our identity keeps us doing countless things over and over again. In the name of "I," we keep making *kammas*—actions with effects—their results unfolding accordingly. The onion is analogous to our constantly unfolding *sankharas*,[37] the ever-changing mental proliferations and self-constructed volitions that we cherish, acting them out here and there, birthed by ignorance and craving, convinced they are the most important thing in the world.[38]

The "I" in this onion is our notion of self. The texts specify three mistaken assumptions resulting from this confusion: "This is mine" (*etam mama*) springs from craving (*tanha*), which gives rise to clinging. "This I am" (*eso'ham asmim*) accords with conceit or self-comparison (*mana*). "This is myself" (*eso me atta*) is personality view (*ditthi*), the deluded concept that there is any lasting or stable version of self. They all impede our freedom.

BIGGER IS NOT BETTER

Here is a short story to illustrate further. In the time of the Buddha lived a monk who was very small in size. Some other monks, those who were unenlightened, teased him by pulling his ears and stroking his head, saying, "How are you, little monk?" Seeing the monks' discourteous behavior, the Buddha said, "This small monk is an arahant who has killed the mother, killed the father, killed both warrior-kings, and destroyed the country along with all its citizens. Now he goes free without any harm."

What did the Buddha mean by that seemingly alarming statement? It was, of course, a teaching metaphor:

> Having slain the mother (craving), the father (self-conceit), two warrior-kings (eternalism and nihilism), and destroyed a country (sense organs and sense objects) together with its treasury (attachment and lust), ungrieving goes the holy man.
>
> Having slain mother, father, two brahmin kings (two extreme views), and a tiger as the fifth (the five mental hindrances), ungrieving goes the holy man.[39]

In this example the concepts represented by mother, father, warrior-kings, the country, and citizens (volitional formations or sankharas)—all are built around the notion of "I."

SEE DHAMMA IN THE BODY

Think of the many, many things you have seen in the course of your lifetime: people, animals, buildings, household objects, movies, plays, trees, flowers, fruits, nuts. We literally cannot count the millions of things we have experienced through the sense of sight. And where are all those things now? All are gone, except in memory.

Just as ephemeral are the emotions we experienced when we saw all those things. How many times did we laugh with joy upon seeing things we enjoyed? Or how many times did we cry or feel anger when seeing sad things such as starving children with their bony bodies, unkempt hair, and sunken eyes?

Think also of the many sounds you have heard in your lifetime: music, speeches, jokes, conversations, quarrels, shouts, cheers, gunshots, car horns. We have all heard sad sounds: someone groaning in pain, crying for help, wailing for a lost loved one. We have felt the sadness that arises when we hear a child crying for its mother or an animal being dragged to slaughter—or, conversely, the thrill of hearing a great symphony played by an orchestra.

Then there is the sense of smell. How many thousands of times have you enjoyed the sweet scent of a rose or the aroma of good food cooking on the stove? Do you remember the unpleasant smells of a sweaty body, dirty socks, or someone's bad breath? Just like the sights and sounds we have experienced, the smells we have experienced are also gone, except in memory. Impermanent, all of it.

We also have memories of taste and touch: delicious food and drinks we have savored, pleasant experiences of touch, a warm breeze on our skin, or the caress of a loved one. And of course, unpleasant experiences, too: bad-tasting food, the slap of a hand on our cheek. All those experiences of taste and touch are now gone, except in memory.

And just as with all those sensory experiences, so too our thoughts and past iterations of consciousness. Millions of thoughts in the course of a lifetime, millions of moments of consciousness. Where are they now? Gone. Vanished. The new ones rise and fall in this very moment, as you sit reading this book.

CHAPTER 8

What Lasts?

JUST AS a couple of drops of water poured onto a hot frying pan that has been left on the stove would evaporate, when mindfulness is established, sensory input, feelings, memories, and mental states all vanish very quickly. The sizzling-hot griddle is like well-established mindfulness. It repels the urge to hold on to anything that cannot provide lasting satisfaction. Is there any form, feeling, memory, or mental state that is not subject to change? When you see absolutely that all such phenomena depend upon ever-changing circumstances, you know that any happiness based upon them is merely provisional. Looking carefully, you can see that even *I, me,* and *my self* are merely concepts pieced together in the mind from fleeting bits of information. They, too, are transitory, impermanent. They dissolve every fraction of a second.

Seeing that so-called personal feelings, perceptions, thoughts, and even consciousness are changing every moment could be disconcerting, but this realization is an opportunity. Remember that you are in an advantageous position to notice all of these happenings as they unfold in your very own mind and body. Where else would you get such a front-row seat to this show? Every thought, perception, feeling, and memory arises depending upon something else related to those thoughts, perceptions, feelings, and memories. The view of them all is most clear from within your body. None of them arises independently. You and only you can notice this.

What we generally assume to be solid is in flux. When you see this for yourself you can lighten up with regard to any mental activity. You know that every possible stressor actually hinges upon some other aspect of being. There is no one person or thing to blame and no single place to send the thank-you notes.

Ignorance, for instance, is impermanent. That is why we can become wise with practice. Thoughts are impermanent. That is how creative solutions emerge. Volitional urges are impermanent. That is why we can change our habits. Their impermanent nature always creates space for the development of wisdom. When any small degree of ignorance fades away a corresponding small degree of wisdom arises in you. That wisdom, having arisen, leads to peace, and peace is all that lasts.

Twenty Types of Self

Is there any enduring self in us? We tend to think so in our materially focused way of thinking, but the Buddha was very firm on this subject. In the *Anattalakkhana Sutta* he did not waver on this point. "Bhikkhus," said the Buddha, "Form is not-self. If form were self, then form would not be prone to affliction, and it would be possible to say: 'Let my form be thus; let my form not be thus.' Because form is not-self, form is prone to affliction, and it is not possible to say, 'Let my form be thus; let my form not be thus.'"[40]

Form is not entirely under our control, even though we put energy into acting as if it were. If this thing called the body were a self, would it not behave according to our liking? Likewise, the mind: if the self wants it to be still, then why are there so many awkward stray thoughts?

Conventionally, we think about the existence of a self, or soul, in four ways: that the physical body is our self, that the body is in our self or owned by our self, that our self is wrapped up in the body, or that a "thing" such as the body and our self are one and the same.[41] When these four ways of thinking about self are multiplied by the five types of aggregates—body, feelings, perceptions, thoughts, and consciousness—and all their possible iterations into manifold phenomena (*sabbe dhamma*), we come up with twenty ways of thinking about self. In the *Sabbasava Sutta* the Buddha called these ways of conceptualizing a "thicket of views."[42]

1. The body is self.	2. The body is in self.	3. Self is in the body.	4. Thus, body and self are identical.
5. Feeling is self.	6. Feeling is in self.	7. Self is in feeling.	8. Thus, feeling and self are identical.
9. Perception is self.	10. Perception is in self.	11. Self is in perception.	12. Thus, perception and self are identical.
13. Volitional formations are self.	14. Volitional formations are in self.	15. Self is in volitional formations.	16. Thus, volitional formations and self are identical.
17. Consciousness is self.	18. Consciousness is in self.	19. Self is in consciousness.	20. Thus, consciousness and self are identical.[43]

REPLACING SELF WITH IMPERMANENCE

The Buddha, however, replaced the concept of self with impermanence, and thus he arrived at the unique concept of anatta, or non-self. The table on the following page shows how that same template would appear when applied to the five aggregates.

According to the *Dhammapada Commentary*, a traditional explanation of the verses in the *Dhammapada*, the Buddha's statement *sabbe dhamma anatta* means that all five aggregates are inherently selfless *dhammas*—phenomena.[44] In other words our body, feelings, perceptions, thoughts, and consciousnesses are all Dhamma. Everything that we know is happening in accord with Dhamma. Everything that we experience is Dhamma. All aggregated phenomena—dhammas—are conditioned (*sankhata*), which means that they all arise in dependence upon causes

1. The body is impermanent.	2. The body is endowed with impermanence.	3. Impermanence is in the body.	4. Thus, body and impermanence are identical.
5. Feeling is impermanent.	6. Feeling is endowed with impermanence.	7. Impermanence is in feeling.	8. Thus, feeling and impermanence are identical.
9. Perception is impermanent.	10. Perception is endowed with impermanence.	11. Impermanence is in perception.	12. Thus, perception and impermanence are identical.
13. Volitional formations are impermanent.	14. Volitional formations are endowed with impermanence.	15. Impermanence is in volitional formations.	16. Thus, volitional formations and impermanence are identical.
17. Consciousness is impermanent.	18. Consciousness is endowed with impermanence.	19. Impermanence is in consciousness.	20. Thus, consciousness and impermanence are identical.

and conditions. As supporting circumstances change, these phenomena pass away dependently as well.

All of them are in a state of flux. These five aggregates constantly wear out because they are impermanent. As they wear out, they must be renewed so they can survive until they become unrenewable. This is the nature of all sankharas, all conditioned things. Your shoes wear out. Your dishwasher wears out. Your car wears out. Your body wears out. Your feelings wear out. All these things must be repaired, renewed, and amended. This wearing out, this flow of change, is taking place all the time. This much is undeniably visible right now if we look with unbiased attention.

The Buddha recommended that we begin by recognizing this change just as it is. He asked us to get intimately close with this impermanence and to observe it with wisdom, thus the invitation to "come and see." And it is not hard to see if we pay attention: impermanence manifests in myriad ways in our bodies and our lives.

Look at the impermanent aggregates of emotion, for example, to see how this plays out in our relationships. When the mind is influenced by anger, hate, jealousy, confusion, and greed, relationships can degenerate from harmony to animosity and rivalry. Friends fight with friends. Children fight with parents. Parents fight with children. Siblings fight with siblings. Relatives fight with relatives. Teachers fight with students. Students fight with teachers. Meditators fight with meditators. Dhamma teachers fight with Dhamma teachers. Men fight with women. Women fight with men. Boys fight with girls. Girls fight with boys. Boys fight with boys. Girls fight with girls. Neighbors fight with neighbors. Ethnic groups fight with ethnic groups. Nations fight with nations.

Let us remember that the harmonious converse can also be true.

People who truly "come and see" Dhamma will understand this situation within themselves. There will be a natural turning away from unwholesome conditioning and an interest in fostering conditions for wholesome aggregates to arise. But one who only learns and teaches Dhamma as an academic subject will never "come and see" Dhamma in the sense of actually understanding how impermanence operates in our lives. We can have Dhamma in our mouths, by talking about it, and also on paper or a computer screen, by reading about it, but if we do not truly investigate it in our own lives, it cannot help us. If we do not "come and see," how can we ever benefit from the very Dhamma that we have in our minds?

Pali has a term for those who relate to Dhamma only in an academic way: *padaparama.* This literally means one for whom "words are paramount." A padaparama only reads and writes Dhamma books, preaches Dhamma, discusses Dhamma, and participates in Dhamma conferences. A padaparama may even count the number of discourses that the Buddha delivered and count the number of words in each. But to read and discuss is much different than to truly "come and see": perhaps nothing has been seen. Let direct experience be paramount. Let us not be padaparamas.

Instead, let us strive to see what is happening to us and within us. Look carefully at the constant change taking place in your mind and body. There is no way to stop this flow of change. It starts from the moment you are conceived in your mother's womb. We have different names for this change. Sometimes we call it growth, sometimes old age, decay, or death. But actually we are dying every moment. You could call it momentary death. Cells in your body die through a programmed biological process called *apoptosis*, and new cells are born in you, over and over. Every feeling dies and new feelings arise. Every perception dies and new perceptions arise. Every thought dies and new thoughts arise. Every moment of consciousness dies and new moments of consciousness arise. Whether or not any buddha comes into the world, this Dhamma is the way things are. This is what you can "come and see."

VENERABLE EMPTY SCRIPTURE

Those of us who simply read and write Dhamma books or listen to Dhamma sermons without investigating further are like Venerable Pothila, a learned monk in the time of the Buddha and a popular spiritual teacher with many students. His knowledge of Dhamma was impressive, his ethical conduct sterling. He was content with any kind of robes, alms food, lodging, and medicines. In short, he was a respected bhikkhu. But he failed to achieve any of the supramundane attainments that might be expected of such a dedicated monk. He had not destroyed his mental defilements.

Wishing to arouse spiritual urgency in Venerable Pothila and understanding his potential for enlightenment, the Buddha called him "Tucca Pothila," which means "empty-headed Pothila." As Pothila approached him, the Buddha would say, "Empty-headed Pothila, how are you?"

or "Empty-headed Pothila, come here," or "Sit down, empty-headed Pothila."

The learned and wise monk Pothila was not angered by the Buddha's seeming insult. Instead, he thought, "I am a popular teacher. My knowledge of Dhamma is deep. So why is the Buddha calling me 'empty-headed?' Maybe it is because I do not meditate. Let me do something about that."

One day, after teaching his students, he left the monastery without telling anyone where he was going. He walked many miles until he entered a forest, and there he found thirty young monks sitting in meditation. Venerable Pothila approached the oldest monk, knelt before him with folded palms, and said, "Please teach me how to meditate."

"Venerable sir," said the young monk, "please do not embarrass me. You are an eminent teacher. Please ask another monk." So Pothila knelt before the next monk in seniority and repeated his request. That monk, too, sent him on, and so on and so forth, until Pothila had asked almost all thirty monks and been refused by each one. Finally he knelt before the youngest monk in the group, a novice. The novice too pointed out Venerable Pothila's learned reputation and begged him not to cause embarrassment by asking him to teach Venerable Pothila how to meditate. In utter desperation Pothila said, "I came all the way here to learn meditation. Please help me. Please teach me how to meditate."

To humble Venerable Pothila and build momentum in him, this novice monk asked, "Do you see that pond over there?"

"Yes, I do," he replied.

"Then get in the pond and listen to me very carefully."

Without a word, Venerable Pothila lowered himself, robes and all, into the pond.

The novice then directed Pothila to get out of the pond. "Venerable sir," he said, "suppose there is an anthill with six holes in it. Suppose a lizard crawls into the anthill. How are you going to catch him?"

Venerable Pothila said, "I would close five of the holes in the anthill and wait until the lizard comes out of the sixth hole. Then I would catch him."

"Similarly, venerable sir," said the novice, "if you restrain five of your six senses—eyes, ears, nose, tongue, and body—and keep your mind focused on your breath, you will notice how all of the aggregates—form, feelings, perceptions, thoughts, and consciousness—change. You will become aware that breath is changing and feeling is changing. As breath comes and goes through your nostrils, feeling arises and passes away. Your attention on the breath and your awareness of the breath changes. This awareness of impermanence opens the door to insight into the reality that everything is unsatisfactory and there is no permanent entity called a self. Eventually your mind will become calm and peaceful, and you will gain concentration. Concentration deepens your insight into the attainment of liberation."[45]

Very wise as he was, Venerable Pothila followed the novice's instructions and soon attained full enlightenment. He looked within, instead of in books, and found truth. "Tucca Pothila" finally became a spiritually full person by recognizing noble qualities within himself. He had actually had those qualities for years, but because he was busy teaching he had had no time to practice meditation. Despite his great knowledge and popularity he was so humble that he was willing to sit in front of a young novice monk and learn meditation from him, just like a little boy learning his lessons sitting with his teacher. And we all must learn to look within ourselves to find the valuable treasure we have there. Then we will find what lasts: peace.

CHAPTER 9

Do Not Look to Somebody Else for the Dhamma in You

AS HE LAY dying, the Buddha uttered these words: "Be an island unto yourself; do not look for another to be an island for you. Be a refuge unto yourself; do not seek another as refuge."[46] Remember the story of the quail, and how safe it was when it returned to its home domain? You could also think of that territory of protection as your *gocara*, the field where cows live and graze. We are like those cows, only rather than grass, we consume forms at the sense doors and thoughts in the field of the mind. If we stay centered within the ancestral domain of the heart, if we nourish ourselves in a well-demarcated, carefully guarded pasture (*satipatthana gocara*)—namely, our own four foundations of mindfulness, being mindful of our bodies, feelings, mental states, and phenomena—we will be fine.

TRY IT, YOU MIGHT LIKE IT

When you look within, you discover Dhamma in yourself: the good, the bad, the beautiful, the ugly. Everything is included in the awareness that knows Dhamma. Although your experience is generally a mixed bag, you will be happy that you are not cruel, do not kill living beings, and do not take what has not been given freely to you, and that you do not abuse your senses. This kind of seeing feeds a self-adjusting process that nourishes what is lovely and skillful. Unwholesome habitual patterns begin to drop away.

You will be happier and happier about your use of words, content in not speaking falsehoods, thankful not to use malicious speech, satisfied without any need for harsh language, and pleased not to engage in gossip. You will feel a greater sense of well-being regarding your mental attitudes, too: it feels good not to be covetous or harbor ill will.

Whether or not you are conscious of these feedback loops, gradually enriching the input will generate more wholesome output. Your inquiry cannot help but begin to bear fruit. When you hold right view, operating from a basic awareness of cause and effect, you give rise to right intention, tend toward right speech, do right action, follow right livelihood, make right effort, practice right mindfulness, and develop right concentration. Directing the mind in this way, you cultivate the eight aspects of the noble eightfold path.

Since the conditions for calm build on themselves and make you glad, you will fall quite naturally into contemplation. As you reflect, a succession of insight knowledges arises seemingly of its own accord. With right knowledge, you are well on your way to the ultimate: right release from suffering.

As insight becomes alive in you, your path toward freedom will straighten out. You will find that you are unlulled by sloth and torpor, less agitated, and less restless. You will be released from doubt and relinquish anger. Eventually you will become totally unencumbered by negative mental states and will no longer be resentful, contemptuous, insolent, or envious. You will then have no avarice, being neither fraudulent nor deceitful, obstinate nor arrogant.

Having tasted the ease and pleasure resulting from meditating in this way, you will feel an urge toward inner and outer harmony. Your inner investigator will not be seduced by fuss or fascination. Your mind will do what needs to be done, without sticking to any object in the world. You will be easy to admonish and have good friends. You will be diligent, faithful, and imbued with a healthy fear of wrongdoing. You will accomplish great learning and accumulate wisdom. Energetic and established in mindfulness, you will not cling tenaciously to your own views, and you will relinquish them when necessary.

These qualities make you happy because you know that you are making the best use of your life and not wasting it. When you "come and see" the direct experience of impermanence inside yourself, you find you are full of great spiritual wealth.

Many years ago a man invited me to conduct a meditation retreat in the country where he lived. But before the retreat was to begin he told me that he had cancelled the event. I later heard that he had pocketed the money collected from the people who had registered for the retreat. I also heard that some time thereafter he was crossing a busy street one day while reading my book *Mindfulness in Plain English*. Because he was not paying attention to his surroundings he was hit by a car and seriously injured. The irony is that in his hands he held a book about mindfulness, but it was not in his mind to "come and see." This is something like a cowherd who looks after somebody else's cattle without having a chance to taste the ghee and butter produced from those cows' milk. Or perhaps it is akin to someone who kicks a piece of gold or a diamond out of his way, unable to see what it is. An ox yoked to a cartload of precious gems might have no knowledge of the value it pulls with its mighty strength all the while.

With our human capacities, we should strive to be different from that ox. We can realize the Dhamma we carry in our minds and bodies—a precious load, right here and now. Recognizing this, its wonders become weightless.

Your Inner Theater

When we look inside ourselves in the spirit of mindfulness, we appreciate that everything is constantly changing. Even though this change is happening all the time, we still might not attune our attention to touch each of those changing moments. This takes practice. It is possible, however, to see moments in time as if they were a sequence of frames in an old-fashioned, reel-to-reel movie. With your inner gaze you can perceive objects of mind as if a strobe light were shone upon them. This is not imagined; rather, it is a capacity of directed meditative acuity.

Snap your finger and you see your finger as your form. You hear the snapping sound. You feel the touch of skin on skin. Almost instantaneously, with trained attention, you can sense a very subtle but powerful physiological cascade that is pleasant, unpleasant, or neither. You recognize the finger, sound, skin, touch, and snap as if on the verge of naming them. You also have a thought about snapping your finger: that is a volitional formation. And you have a conscious moment of the snapping itself. In this simple, quick action of snapping your finger, all the five aggregates—form, feeling, perception, volitional formations, and consciousness—work together in concert. All of them appear and disappear very quickly. It is possible to touch each of these five steps directly with your attention, without resorting to scholarship or philosophy. This experience of reality is absolutely accessible and exactly what is meant by "come and see."

In approaching this nature of ever-changing Dhamma (literally "seeing Dhamma by way of the body") so closely, it is possible to become one with it. As if you were inside a turning kaleidoscope, you can see the body as it is and thus know all things as they are. Becoming intimate with the aggregates, you can see their allure, but you can also see their temporary natures and the danger in succumbing to their attraction. The three key features of conditioned phenomena, and even of the consciousness that detects phenomena—impermanence, suffering, and inherent selflessness—all make themselves apparent. Continually perceiving this, you are established in Dhamma. This is what the Buddha referred to when he invited us to "come and see."

When the senses come into contact with sensory objects, a series of thought moments arises. They may turn out to be lustful thoughts or hateful thoughts, jealous thoughts, fearful thoughts, thoughts of cruelty, even tepid or vapid or totally unremarkable thoughts. Hopefully we recognize these thoughts at the very moment they arise and can feel them as they arise and pass away. The meeting of senses and sensory objects is Dhamma. The feeling arising from that contact is Dhamma. Thoughts arising from that contact are Dhamma. Reaction to the thoughts is Dhamma. We can see it all happening right within ourselves. We want to be fully engaged in knowing this process, intimately involved in it all. This is "come and see."

When greed arises, for example, we experience pain. When greed fades away we feel relief from that pain. We strive to "come and see" the very nature of greed and the felt sense of the absence of greed. Similarly, when hatred arises we feel pain, and when hatred fades away we experience joy. We can "come and see" the very nature of hatred and joy. When fear, tension, worry, or anxiety arise, we are in pain, and when those feelings disappear we are relieved of the pain. We want to "come and see" the very nature of all these mental states.

In other words, paying total mindful attention to what is happening within us is the essence of "come and see." When we see someone we like or hear a loved one's voice, we are happy. When we eat delicious food, drink our favorite drink, or smell something delightful, we are happy. We are happy to touch things or people we like. We are happy even imagining the things or people we like. We are happy to be with what and whom we like. But this happiness is conditional.

When pleasant emotions change to unpleasant ones, we experience unhappiness. When we lose sight of our loved ones, we are unhappy. When we cannot hear what we like to hear, we are unhappy. When we cannot smell things we like, we are unhappy. When we cannot eat or drink what we like, we are unhappy. When we cannot touch or be with whatever or whomever we like, we are unhappy. When our minds seem blocked from generating good thoughts, we are unhappy then, too. And this sort of unhappiness is also conditional.

We must ask ourselves why we cannot stop the repeated ending of what we find so likeable or the return of unsolicited unpleasant experience.

Why must we part from all that we hold dear? Why does it seem that we can never completely rid ourselves of what is unwanted? The answer will inevitably be some variation of "because things change and because we change" or perhaps "because the situation has changed." Of course, we know that changes in circumstance can trigger a switch from happy to unhappy and vice versa. We see it in real-time. We also see that there is nothing we can do to prevent these changes from happening. Unhappiness arises by wishing to stop the change of what is pleasant and wishing to prevent the unpleasantness from taking place. Our greed to possess the pleasant and our greed to reject the unpleasant always make for conflict. Greed is the source of so much of our pain. This greed is our suffering. And trying to satisfy our insatiable desire is always suffering.

Despite our earnest wish, we cannot truly grasp or reject anything. Grasping and clinging is mere wishing. We are simply attempting to grasp or reject, and we fail because everything is changing so rapidly. Before we can even attempt to grasp or reject something or someone, it has changed in the blink of an eye.

But if our mind is free from the wish to grasp or reject, even for a fraction of a second, we experience peace. Only when we recognize that fact utterly and completely does a natural and sustained letting go ensue effortlessly. We must "come and see" that we experience peace when greed or hatred is abandoned even for an instant; we must "come and see" that we experience pain in each moment when we have mental impurities or unconscious confusion about what really matters. And when those mental impurities are cleansed, we experience peace and happiness.

You can link these moments of freedom together and reside there. This is the treasure of your body and mind: they actually invite us to "come and see" Dhamma. We do not need anybody else to ask us to look. We must expend the effort ourselves, look inside and experience this nature of Dhamma, understand it, and clearly comprehend the unfolding phenomena we find there. We can understand how things come to be—not because someone told us, but because we see for ourselves. We must cultivate the habit to "come and see" what is really going on in this body and mind, without trying to point a finger at others. Pointing a finger at others is the opposite of the principle of "come and see."

Self-examination and looking into the personal mind is a much more effective way of correcting yourself than relying on others. This is how we practice mindfulness of the mind and of our vacillating mental states. This is how we learn what can be controlled and what cannot. This is how we become familiar with what gives rise to our assorted states of mind. We "come and see" everything appearing and disappearing, and these appearances and disappearances aren't just what we have in us. They are us.

Often our habitual knowledge of what happens to others is inferential, not direct (not *sanditthika*), not personally realizable by a wise individual (not *paccatabbam veditabbo vinnuhi*). We do not know for sure because we are not inside their minds. But we can shift this habit. From time to time, we can ask ourselves *if* we are sure. We can discern what is really happening and what is a secondarily arising conceptual overlay; we can know the difference between that which truly is and the stories we tell ourselves. We can recognize that which is unornamented, unembellished, unadorned before we speak or act. This is wonderful psychological and mental training. It urges us to be mindful of the three principles of phenomena happening directly in our own minds and bodies—impermanence, suffering, and not a separate self.

The Buddha realized this truth and taught it to the world; then he passed away. Now it is up to us. We can experience this eternal truth at any moment in this very life. Nobody, no god, no human, no Mara, can turn impermanence into permanence, suffering into non-suffering, or non-self into self. Impermanence remains impermanence, suffering remains suffering, and non-self remains non-self. Seeing this with wisdom, we liberate ourselves from the suffering of believing otherwise.

We should use the mind and its contents as a laboratory for testing our mindfulness. Suppose we dream that we are separated from a loved one. When this painful parting of ways happens in a dream, in the beginning it is difficult to be mindful. And when we wake up from the dream of separation, we worry because of our attachment to our loved one. But if we train ourselves in every waking moment to be mindful, a dream of separation would not worry us. We can perform this training on ourselves, in the personal laboratory of life experience, even without a lab assistant.

NOT ME, NOT MINE, NOT WHO I AM

Our experience of body and mind is constantly changing, with states arising and passing away all the time. If we "come and see," we find that all experiences are impermanent and unsatisfactory. Their nature is to arise, to change, to fade away. Phenomena that depend upon changing circumstances as their supports are of the nature to fade, a nature that is ungraspable. All transitory things cease by their very nature, being always contingent, conditioned; this nature is called *dependent origination*. They are not mine. I am not they. They are not my self.

Seeing all conditioned experiences in this way, we become disenchanted with them. Disenchantment, despite the negative connotation of the word, is an excellent state of being. It arises from a deep realization of the truth. It is, in fact, the most optimistic, spiritually uplifting experience we can have. Being disenchanted, we become dispassionate. A dispassionate state of mind is very calm, functioning in the healthiest manner. The healthy mind that deeply understands the truth of how things are will be liberated from greed, hatred, and delusion. The liberated mind knows the exhaustion of the possibility for any future births. It knows that what was to be done has been done and that nothing more remains to be done.

CONVENTIONAL TRUTHS, ETERNAL TRUTHS

Even though we use words such as *I, my,* and *myself* in everyday life, we know that in reality they do not exist. As with Sunday, Monday, January, February, latitude, and longitude, they are concepts for cooperatively navigating the world: in reality, mere ideas. They are not solid entities.

In 1985 I visited the Fiji Islands. While we were walking along a road one day, our tour guide said, "If you step to the right side of the road, you will be in yesterday. If you step to the left side of the road, you will be in tomorrow. But here, walking down the middle of this road, you are in today." It turned out that we were standing on the International Date Line. No one has ever actually seen an International Date Line; it is imaginary. But we understand the concept. We evoke it when it is useful and then let it go.

Convention tends to hide eternal truth. What can we do about that? As long as we live in conventional society we have to use certain agreed-upon terms, even though the objects they signify are not necessarily real. And even though we know this, many of these ideas get us into trouble. Similarly, any time we say, "This is mine," craving arises in us. When we say, "This is me," conceit arises in us. When we say, "This is my self," what the Buddha called *wrong view* arises. They are all perspectives not in accord with the way things are, convenient but provisional truths.

Here is a story to illustrate what happens to us when we do not "come and see" the workings of our minds:

One day, someone brought a delicious offering of cooked fish to a temple. In that temple lived one monk and one young boy who served as the monk's assistant. When the monk sat down to eat, the boy offered him the whole dish. In it were eight small pieces of fish. The monk took three at once.

As the monk ate, the boy watched attentively. He thought, "Well, he is a monk and the head of this temple. I must respect him. Let him have three pieces. There are five more. That is enough for my lunch and dinner."

When the monk finished eating, he stretched out his hand to pick up more fish.

The boy thought, "Surely he deserves half of this dish. Let him have one more." But the monk took two pieces of fish.

The boy thought, "Never mind; let him have five pieces. There are still three left. That is plenty for me."

After eating the two pieces, the monk helped himself to two more, leaving only one small piece of fish in the dish.

The boy thought, "Never mind. I am small. He is big. One piece is enough for me."

But then the monk reached for the very last piece of fish—and the boy's patience ran out.

"Venerable sir," he cried. "Are you going to eat this last piece of fish without leaving anything for me?"

In his greed for the delicious fish, the monk was unmindful and had totally forgotten his faithful assistant, waiting patiently to have his meal. The monk was so embarrassed that, ever after, he refrained from eating greedily.[47]

If you "come and see" faithfully, if you keep watch over your mind and its contents, you will recognize whether your mind is greedy or not greedy, hateful or not hateful, deluded or not deluded, contracted and distracted or not contracted and distracted, developed or not developed, concentrated or not concentrated—and thus, liberated or not liberated.

Walking, sitting, standing, going forward, returning, bending your arms and legs, stretching them, wiggling fingers and toes, eating, drinking, even answering the call of nature, we can see impermanence very clearly. But to see this we have to look. We do not have to ask anybody to teach this Dhamma because it is right here in the body, showing us the very nature of all that is, intrinsic, incontrovertible. Everything in us and around us is made of and marked by change.

CHAPTER 10

A Practical Exercise for Anywhere

LET US APPLY these principles of "come and see" to vipassana practice, where they show their true power to reveal Dhamma in any situation. We can start with the three unwholesome roots. Suppose you are sitting on your meditation cushion and a craving for something arises in your mind. What should you do? First, acknowledge that if there were no tendency toward craving in your mind, craving would not have arisen. Although your mind is luminous, it is not totally pure. Next, recognize that there is a very real possibility of liberating your mind from craving. Then observe your thoughts without following them until the craving fades away.

When the craving ends, recognize that it has gone. Cultivate these thoughts: "How wonderful! This mind was full of craving before. Now there is none. That means I have the chance to liberate this mind from craving."

Finally, reflect on the nature of a craving-free mind. It is generous, gentle, compassionate, and happy to renounce thoughts of sensual pleasure. With this confidence, you proceed.

Suppose some other time, while you are meditating, you hear sounds around you. Another meditator, perhaps, is doing walking meditation and the floor keeps creaking loudly. Someone else coughs. A third person sneezes. Then someone actually starts snoring.

You become irritated and think, "Why can that person not walk quietly? Why does that other person not take some cough medicine? Why does the person sitting next to the snoring person not wake him up?"

Angry thoughts crowd into your mind. Aversion arises, maybe even hatred.

When you recognize that aversion and hatred have arisen, you can think, "Hateful thoughts have arisen in me." You can also reflect on how hatred arises depending on causes or conditions, how unpredictable it is. Try not to personalize it by thinking, "My mind is full of hatred." If you have to conceptualize, try "the mind" instead of "my mind." Better yet, just feel without sticking to what is happening, without making up stories or explanations or plans. Words block awareness of what is going on in the mind. Simply pay attention and notice what has arisen as having arisen.

As you maintain the awareness that aversion is not personal, that it arises dependent upon causes or conditions, you can use mindfulness techniques to overcome these angry, hate-filled thoughts. As before, pay attention to the thoughts without following them. Observe the impact of hatred on your consciousness. And then reflect on the nature of a hate-free mind—how beautiful, peaceful, and relaxed it is.

As for working with delusion, it is less noticeable. The mind must be free from delusion to understand that it is free from delusion. Before delusion arises in your mind, the mind is clear, in the same way that before you fall asleep, you are awake. All you need to do at that moment is pay attention to the fact that your mind is clear.

When you pay attention to that which is not deluded, the clouds of delusion slowly fade away and the clear, sky-like mind appears again. You see that consciousness is always changing. Thoughts arise and disappear in that space of mind. They are impermanent. When delusion arises, you pay attention to it for only as long as it is strongly compelling, knowing that it is a delusion. Then, because everything changes, your focus eventually opens up, and the arisen disturbing quality of delusion fades away. Once again, you know the mind as clear, aware, luminous.

Letting Go of My Greed, Hatred, and Cruelty

The four noble truths of Buddhism propose that we ponder four things: the truth of suffering, the cause of suffering, the end of suffering, and the steps needed to end suffering. To profit from these points we have to "come and see" what this notion means within ourselves.

Suffering does not have an owner. It simply exists, within me, within you. To be free, I must look at my experience of that suffering honestly when it arises. Then I must try to understand how I can divest myself of this suffering by cultivating right thought.

If I think with greed, I suffer. So I try to think thoughts of generosity, which help me to let go of greed and reduce my suffering. If I have hateful thoughts, I suffer. So I try to think thoughts of loving-friendliness, which help me to let go of hatred and reduce my suffering. If I think cruel thoughts, I suffer. So I try to think thoughts of compassion, which help me to let go of my cruelty and reduce my suffering.

Thinking about letting go of my greed, hatred, and cruelty just occasionally is not enough to benefit from the practice. I must think of letting go of them every day, every hour, and every minute. Even then, in spite of my earnest wish, they may arise. Then I must think about overcoming them, subduing them, overpowering them, weakening them, rebuking them, and removing them.

Generosity helps me to let go of greed. When I cultivate and nourish thoughts of generosity, I strangle and suffocate greed. Loving-friendliness helps me to let go of hatred. When I cultivate and nourish thoughts of loving-friendliness, I strangle and suffocate hatred. Compassion helps me to let go of cruelty. When I cultivate and nourish thoughts of compassion, I strangle and suffocate cruelty.

Of course, my tradition has a reputation for being kind to people and all sorts of creatures, but the texts use strong language for working with afflictive emotions. When I am fully present to recognize my difficulty as it is, that is kindness. This includes an honest acknowledgment of the suffering without repressing it. By *strangle*, I mean that I stop pouring life into thoughts that are purely unhelpful. By *suffocate*, I mean stifling the needless perpetuation of difficulty. In this way, while not harming the actual physical object of my thinking or feeling, I simply do not give energy to further unwholesome thoughts. When they are deprived of my personal power to fuel them, the thoughts simply deflate. By not building upon them, I do not make things worse for myself or anyone else.

This practice can support your mindfulness training. As you let go of your greed, hatred, and cruelty and instead practice generosity, friendliness, and compassion, you become more mindful. As mindfulness increases, the first outwardly noticeable change often involves speech. You might speak softly and more cordially, or at least with a tone that is not so sharp. With continued practice you might find that you always tell the truth, do not malign anyone, and say only meaningful things. Using speech in this way, you experience happiness and reduce your suffering as well as that of others. This in turn will affect action, thought, and even livelihood.

As for your actions, you naturally abstain from stealing and sexual misconduct because you cannot bring yourself to condition painful outcomes. You show your friendliness and compassion to all living beings, and you delight in others' good health and happiness. You also choose a vocation in which you can work together with others in friendliness and compassion.

Thus your understanding, effort, and mindfulness become strong. As they become strong, your wholesome thoughts, speech, action, livelihood, and concentration become stronger, too. With strong concentration you can see your suffering even more clearly than before. You can also start to see the way out. Thus you go on repeating the practice of these eight steps, which comprise the Buddha's noble eightfold path. Each and every time you repeat them, your thoughts, speech, action, livelihood, effort, mindfulness, and concentration become purer and purer, more refined, until finally you overcome your ego, which is none other than the notion of an enduring self.

EXPIRATION DATE

Speaking of that which does not endure, we must keep in mind the fact that everything has an expiration date. We are born with an expiration date. All things that begin expire by default. Biochemistry can trace our expiration dates. If you can estimate how many cells get born in our bodies and how long each cell can live, then you will be able to predict that date. Sometimes this date can be postponed. However, eventually we will not be able to extend the warranty. The oxygen-carrying capacity of our blood also has a default expiration date, and the marrow generates replacement red cells to replenish its healthy function. Even our skeletons have cells whose main job is to break down bone, and there are other cells whose responsibility is to build new bone from the delicate and ever-changing balance of minerals within the blood. When bodily systems can no longer refurbish themselves at a rate that keeps pace with their degeneration, this is the date beyond which you cannot extend your life. That is your physiological expiration date.

When you are conceived, impermanence is born right along with the moment of conception. Your mother's body usually provides all that is necessary and sufficient for development in the womb. The blueprint and raw materials generously donated by your parents inform and supply the constant multiplying of new cells to replace dying cells during the nine-month remodeling process that results in baby you. At birth you emerge, made of trillions of cells. From that moment, there is only becoming and changing, going on and on with a one-way ticket, without a ticket for return, and only until your warranty expires. When you meet with love and compassion, this too brings about becoming and change. You can benefit yourself and others most of all if you "come and see" the reality that everything is impermanent. But you must begin before that warranty expires, and you must continue. As with your physical growth, now is the time to arouse spiritual urgency (*samvega*) and confidence (*pasada*) in order to accelerate the maturation of your mindfulness practice.

WATER IN A DEEP WELL

Biologists, chemists, and physicists, as well as those without knowledge of any science at all, can use human reasoning to understand impermanence by experimenting cognitively with things outside of themselves. Their understanding is like seeing water in a deep well. Water in a deep well cannot necessarily quench your thirst. You have to drink that water to quench your thirst. Your arms and hands are not long enough to reach the water at the bottom of the deep well. Nor do you have a bucket or a rope with which to reach the water. This is an analogy for how most people understand impermanence, intellectually.

Just as you need a bucket and a long rope to get the water, and just as you must actually drink the water yourself in order to quench your thirst, you need to pay total, undivided, mindful attention to one singular something where the impermanence is most conspicuous in order to quench suffering. For the purpose of this exercise, that something is your own breath, which is changing all the time. You notice breath changing by paying very simple attention.

PARADOXICAL PEACE

In this tradition the breath is called a "body-conditioner" (*kayasankhara*). This means that without the vital pre-existing condition of breath happening, the collection of systems that comprises the body would not exist. *Kaya* is a heap of things or parts, and it also means "body." *Sankhara* can mean "formation" or a cluster of seen or unseen things, but in this case it means "substratum." It is a process or collection upon which another process or collection depends. Oxygen brings life to every single cell in our bodies. The breath is the condition for everything else in these bodies to occur.

When you pay careful attention to your ever-changing breath, you actually encounter permanent happiness. That might sound paradoxical, but it is not. For one thing, you cannot find anything permanent; just when you think you have found something permanent, disappointment comes quickly when that thing changes. And for another, when you see impermanence in everything you cannot be disappointed, because you continuously encounter the truth. This sort of truth can never fail.

Only when you try to hide or ignore the truth will you be disappointed. In a moment of rigidity, impermanence inevitably reveals itself. When you forget how insubstantial things really are, impermanence is there, unexpectedly causing you grief, lamentation, and suffering. You cannot fight change, as the opponent would be your own fixed belief. But this may come as a relief when you rest in the flow of experience rather than in the certainty of any object. Because experience flows everywhere, you are at peace anywhere in the world.

When you do not live and act based on the realized wisdom of impermanence, then impermanence is very painful. This pain can be acknowledged or unacknowledged. It could be the subtle angst that lingers when you arrive home from work, a personal interaction that goes awry, or the frustration when things do not go the way you had planned. Small resentment or looming crisis, impermanence does not care, nor is it the cause of the suffering. It is our resistance to it that hurts. No matter how much you argue with the truth of experience, it just is. When you wish for your body, your house, or your car to remain the same forever, you suffer. Instead you can identify with the impermanent nature of aliveness itself, for which there is no insurance policy.

The Laboratory

Some people do research in laboratories. They do this work in external laboratories, clean rooms, petri dishes, or plots in the field or forest. For their respective studies professional researchers might involve various kinds of animals, human beings, insects, snakes, fish, seeds, and plants. They might alter the physical qualities in their experimental environment, such as heat or moisture or light. They might use specific delivery methods like hoses, faucets, gas valves and flames, or electrical sockets, with mechanical or wired devices for measuring and recording. These are external things.

In meditation we use ourselves as our own laboratories and find everything we need for our experiment right within our bodies. To see impermanence this is actually the best workshop possible. The movement of air, the flowing and cohesive qualities of water, the presence or absence of heat, the solidity of earth—the elements are all perfectly observable within this internal apparatus. The physical package each of us was born with provides an opportunity for up-close study of ever-changing feelings, assorted perceptions, arising thoughts, and volitional urges. In the body we can watch myriad processes generating vivid and colorful varieties of consciousness, the non-stop rising and falling of everything, without beginning and without end. We experience all this right here in the body at any given moment.

Traveling

The Buddha agreed that this very human body and life provide exactly what will best inform our mindful investigation all the way to enlightenment. Rohitassa, a deity, once asked the Buddha:

> "Is it possible, Bhante, by traveling to know, see, or reach the end of the world, where one is not born, does not grow old and die, does not pass away and get reborn?"

Answering his question, the Buddha said:

> "I say, friend, that by traveling one cannot know, see, or reach
> that end of the world where one is not born, does not grow old
> and die, does not pass away and get reborn . . . Yet I say that
> without having reached the end of the world there is no mak-
> ing an end of suffering. It is in this fathom-long body endowed
> with perception and mind that I proclaim (1) the world,
> (2) the origin of the world, (3) the cessation of the world, and
> (4) the way leading to the cessation of the world.[48]

You do not need to fly through the sky to some exotic country or sail a
ship across the ocean. Just like Rohitassa, you can look into the world of
your own mind and heart. There you will encounter many lands and an
ocean of loving-kindness. When things get overpopulated in there, only
you can stop generating more content. If the craving to make more and
do more and concoct and construct feels intense, look to see where the
wanting comes from. It is probably not coming from "out there." You can
pay wise and gentle attention right where the stress arises until it runs out
of fuel and stops on its own. You can find restful pleasure in the breath
and adjust your thoughts, words, and deeds to make your situation more
conducive to insight. This is a portable practice. These are transferable
skills. You can do this experiment in any situation, at any time. As you
practice in many unique moments, the attention will naturally become
more refined. The key is remembering to "come and see," and to do so
with kindness.

CHAPTER 11

Infused with Metta

OPTIMAL CONDITIONS

IF WE OPT to travel the inner terrain that leads to the end of the world, there are certain conditions that make the road less bumpy. Mindfulness arises more readily with a certain amount of joy and ease. If we practice friendliness and acceptance toward the world, these qualities visit us spontaneously, and we do not find ourselves distracted by their opposites.

Just as all parents aspire to provide affection, safety, food, education, and a comfortable home for their child, so too can we generate certain inner circumstances that encourage mindfulness to grow straight and tall from a firm foundation. The optimal worldly conditions for the upbringing of mindfulness are called the *brahma viharas*, the four divine abidings. They are *metta*, loving-friendliness or -kindness; *karuna*, compassion; *mudita*, joy for others' good fortune; and *upekkha*, equanimity or inclusiveness.

While all four of these qualities can be practiced to the point of concentration and benefit, they are not the focus of this book. Let us here consider metta, popular among laypeople and monastics alike, and for good reason.

WHERE CAN WE SEE THE BENEFIT OF METTA?

Bhikkhus, there are eleven benefits of the practice of loving-friendliness that arise from the emancipation of the heart if it

is repeated, developed, made much of, made a habit of, made
a basis, experienced, practiced, and well undertaken. What
eleven?

One sleeps well; one gets up well; one does not have night-
mares; one is pleasing to human beings; one is pleasing to non-
human beings; deities protect one; neither fire nor poison nor
a weapon affect one; one's mind becomes calm immediately;
one's complexion brightens; one dies without confusion; and
beyond that, if one does not comprehend the highest, one
goes to the world of the brahmas.[49]

Clearly the situation described in the above passage would facilitate the
practice of mindfulness. The Buddha even said that when we practice
metta, dangers such as fire, poison, and weapons cannot harm us. You
may ask whether this is true. It is. If you practice diligently according to
this metta instruction, you can verify the result for yourself.

All you need to do is pay undivided, impartial attention—infused
with metta. The Buddha said that only when we attend without bias can
we see the truth: "All dhammas become visible to mindful attention"
(*manasikara sambhava sabbe dhamma*).[50] This is another instance where
dhammas means phenomena rather than teachings. It is as if mindful
attention adds a higher-quality lens to our inner vision so that we might
view each experience more intimately. Where do these glimpses present
themselves? Within. Even with metta there is no exception.

NOT ON FIRE

What is the fire that does not harm us when we practice metta? The Buddha described it in the following summary in the *Adittapariyaya Sutta*:

The eye is on fire; forms, eye consciousness, eye contact, and
feeling that arises depending on eye-contact are on fire. The ear

is on fire; sounds, ear-consciousness, ear-contact, and feeling that arises depending on ear-contact are on fire. The nose is on fire; odors, nose-consciousness, nose-contact, and feeling that arises depending on nose-contact are on fire. The tongue is on fire; tastes, tongue-consciousness, tongue-contact, and feeling that arises depending on tongue-contact are on fire. The body is on fire; touch, body-consciousness, body-contact, and feeling that arises depending on body-contact are on fire. The mind is on fire; mental objects, mind-consciousness, mind-contact, and feeling that arises depending on mind-contact are on fire. And with what are these on fire? With the fire of passion, I say, the fire of hatred, the fire of delusion. With birth, old age, death, sorrow, lamentation, pain, grief, and despair they are on fire. This is the summary of the discourse.[51]

We can "come and see" how our fires of passion, hatred, and delusion cannot help but give rise to birth, old age, and death as well as to the sorrow, lamentation, pain, grief, and despair[52] that follow them. And we can perceive firsthand how these same fires are extinguished during the practice of metta. You can realize this truth for yourself.

PREPARING THE FIELD WITH METTA

"One who sees Dhamma sees me."[53] As we ready ourselves for a more comprehensive and sustained application of the tools offered by the Buddha, we might consider his statement as a koan. We can allow the mind to dwell in the pre-conceptual. With metta, we can acknowledge that we do not perceive dependent origination completely and, in so doing, create an opening that both prepares us for and motivates our deeper exploration of impermanence.

Often we hear of people complaining that they cannot practice loving-friendliness meditation. They say that when they begin to explore metta meditation they recall some unpleasant experience from childhood. Actually, this seems like all the more reason to surround oneself with loving-friendliness. Some say that they direct their metta practice toward loved ones—their relatives or friends—very sick in hospitals or homes. In spite of their sincere attempts at well-wishing, their loved ones eventually pass away. Grief-stricken and frustrated, they then either give up the metta practice altogether or begin to complain. This is confusion. What they should really do is look at their own mind to "come and see" whether or not they have understood the real way and meaning of practicing metta.

In the formal teachings on sending metta to others, there is no mention of profit for the recipient of your good wishes. If you generate metta, then you are the one who gains. If your loved ones are suffering from various maladies and you want to offer them the pleasant results of metta, then encourage them to practice metta with you. When they themselves start to engender goodwill, their hearts will transform. Then you both "come and see" internally the effect of loving-friendliness, and you both find what is refreshing and wonderful. Your heart and the hearts of your loved ones will be released from the eleven fires mentioned earlier.

For "the liberation of mind by loving-friendliness," the Buddha recommended that metta be "developed and cultivated, frequently practiced, made one's vehicle and foundation, firmly established, consolidated, and properly undertaken."[54] In other words, your metta should be "made much of, made a habit of, made a basis"[55] of your mindfulness meditation. It is said that if you practice in this way, you will experience certain "benefits of metta, well-undertaken."[56] From the man who proclaimed spiritual friendship to be the entirety of the path, we would expect nothing less than making metta part and parcel with everything.

BASIC CONDITIONS FOR EFFECTIVE METTA

The Buddha's compassionate and wise recommendation is that we develop the following qualities in our minds, and in that way apply metta meditation for attaining the state of peace:

> One skilled in good, wishing to attain
> that state of peace, should act thus:
> One should be able, straight, upright,
> obedient, gentle, and humble.
> One should be content, easy to support,
> with few duties, living lightly,
> controlled in senses, discreet,
> not impudent, unattached to families.
> One should not do any slight wrong
> that the wise might censure.[57]

These lines are the beginning verses of the *Karaniyametta Sutta*, *The Discourse on Loving-Kindness*, which is recited all over the globe, and those who try the above instructions will discover why. If we "come and see" the truth of this statement in ourselves, we see that the Buddha is sitting inside of us and teaching us Dhamma. This sutta is an excellent example of a profound method that we can internalize. As we do this we literally change the world, inside and out, through the cultivation of goodwill. The Buddha uses the term *karaniya* in the sutta, meaning "should be done." This means that in the cultivation of metta, we must be prepared to practice.

Remember that one who genuinely develops such a degree of friendliness will not be affected by fire, poison, or weapons. If we pause to reflect deeply on the fresh and gentle qualities of metta described in the sutta before we actually begin generating it in practice, we see the wisdom and compassion of the Buddha. Seeing the profundity of these two qualities, we see the Buddha himself. This discourse goes on to explain that if we practice metta well, we can live a divine life right here and now on this very earth.

CHAPTER 12

The Map and the Practice

IN THERAVADA BUDDHISM there are said to be ten ties that bind us to samsara.[58] The living tradition, descended from the earliest complete collection of Buddhist teachings, describes four levels of beings with increasing freedom in their hearts and minds with respect to those ten fetters: stream enterers, once returners, non-returners, and arahants.[59] Each of these four entails a momentary experience of nibbana, and they all connote some degree of awakening, culminating in arahantship.

You realize the first stage, stream entry, by practicing the mundane version of the noble eightfold path until you directly experience the impermanence, selflessness, and unsatisfactoriness inherent in all compounded phenomena. The moment you relinquish your ego and banish the notion of an enduring self, you enter the stream of the supramundane path. At this point your practice becomes a supramundane version of the noble eightfold path. With each level of awakening, your right view changes. This newly adjusted path factor, also called right understanding, increasingly attuned to the way things are, will inform the way you relate with the other seven path factors. Once you step into this first clearing on the path, you then proceed toward further disentanglement, and eventually complete freedom.

This is the map, and with it you realize increasing degrees of impermanence. But the map is not the same as the destination. And there are certain places where you can receive a lift or find yourself stuck. Let us consider a few of these.

WE ARE ALL NOBILITY

As we step onto the noble eightfold path, imbued with metta and the other brahma viharas, another aspect of the Buddha's Dhamma carries us right from the start: if metta infuses our practice, merit supports it.

This crucial aspect of the path to liberation from suffering is called *punna kamma*, "the doing of good deeds." It can be divided into three indispensable subsets: *dana*, or generosity; *sila*, or ethical virtue; and *bhavana*, or meditation. Since these categories of activity are almost always listed in this same order, clearly the spirit of giving comes first. After establishing the fundamental underpinnings of sharing and making altruistic donations, we perfect our restraint and non-harmful conduct. Finally we engage in the process of bhavana. This third type of merit-making is often the main activity expected by those new to meditation, but its practice actually rests upon lifetimes of generating goodness and refraining from harm.

Dana is considered the easiest way to make merit, or do good, and it is the first of the *paramis*, or qualities to be perfected leading toward buddhahood. Its presence makes less wholesome qualities such as clinging or stinginess at least momentarily impossible. Gift giving is a cherished form of renouncing, an exercise in letting go.

In the *Dakkhinavibhanga Sutta, The Discourse on the Analysis of Offerings*, there are fourteen types of dana that the Buddha described to his attendant, Ananda:

> One gives a gift to the Tathāgata,[60] accomplished and fully enlightened; this is the first kind of personal offering. One gives a gift to a paccekabuddha[61] ... to an arahant disciple of the Tathāgata ... to one who has entered upon the way to the realization of the fruit of arahantship ... to a non-returner ... to one who has entered upon the way to the realization of the fruit of non-return ... to a once-returner ... to one who has

entered upon the way to the realization of the fruit of once-return . . . to a stream-enterer . . . to one who has entered upon the way to the realization of the fruit of stream-entry . . . to one outside [the Dispensation][62] who is free from lust for sensual pleasures . . . to a virtuous ordinary person . . . to an immoral ordinary person . . . to an animal; this is the fourteenth kind of personal offering.[63]

We are all endowed with the seeds of nobility. Every part of society is included in the list above, even non-human animals. The practice of giving in this tradition leaves no one out and no one behind. In dissolving boundaries between various aspects of society by making offerings, we must necessarily relinquish divisions within ourselves. Giving gifts to the four levels of realized beings, however, is thought to be particularly auspicious.

The state of mind of the individual who makes the offering is important for the highest and best outcome of the gift. The giver should also have obtained the offering in righteous ways before giving it. Growing up in a culture where this wholesome habit prevails means that one may "come and see" the fruits of making such offerings from an early age. Stepping onto the noble eightfold path grounded in the spirit of dana makes for a comprehensive entry into the experience of impermanence.

Sticking Points

Once you set out in earnest on the path to freedom, with your bodily actions established in goodness and restraint and your mind infused with metta, your concentration will deepen. All sorts of unusual phenomena may or may not arise at this juncture. The reality that once seemed solid will disintegrate or even seem to shatter; this can happen gradually or suddenly.

Some meditators encounter new sensations in the body. You might feel the urge to sway and move around. You might be tempted to analyze and invent personal stories to explain the feelings. Remember that all of these are simply potential sources of distraction. If you wish for such physical effects, recognize this wanting. If you wish for them to go away, recognize this aversion.

Liberation is like an unbinding or unwinding; it is a process that you can experience in the body for yourself. The parts of you that you do not currently perceive as empty and impermanent will unravel. You should treat whatever feeling arises as you would any other mental object. Then return to the breath. Fascination with experiences along the path to freedom is not freedom itself.

Likewise, with thoughts, some people get mixed up in their own questions when studying the map of spiritual development. They forget their goal of freedom. They forget to practice looking inward and think themselves in circles instead. They ask, for instance, "Why are there four separate stages of enlightenment?" The second stage, the once returner, seems particularly confusing. The description does not specify how much greed and hatred should be reduced to enter the once returner's path, and likewise later for the once returner's fruition. Since a person finally destroys greed and hatred only when they enter the third stage of enlightenment, some people think that perhaps there were only three stages in the Buddha's original teaching. They surmise that the unspecified second stage was added later on, the historicity of which can confuse things.

Such people might consult Pali commentaries, some of which add more confusion by stating that the path and fruition aspects of each stage are attained within two thought moments of one another, without acknowledging much time to cultivate the path to the attainment of fruition. If the path and fruition aspects of each successive step are attained only two brief thought moments apart from one another, then in normal time and space there is no way a person could have the time to give gifts to those on the paths of the stream enterer, once returner, non-returner, and arahant as recommended by the Buddha in his *Dakkhinavibhanga Sutta*. And even this line of thinking conflicts with a teaching from another source. This can easily become an exercise in mental cogitation that subjects the thinker to further confusion.

Once again, the best answer seems to be to "come and see." If you see for yourself, there will be little reason to debate about mental constructs. The same goes for great existential questions that might arise. In the *Culamalunkya Sutta, The Shorter Discourse to Malunkyaputta,* the Buddha uses the simile of the poisoned arrow to show the venerable Malunkyaputta[64] that there are certain cosmic questions not worth answering—they do not lead to the goal. Do not get distracted from the path to freedom. Inform your study with real practice. You can do it. The Buddha never asked us to do anything that we cannot do:

> "Bhikkhus, cultivate skillfulness. It is possible to cultivate skillfulness. If it were not possible to cultivate skillfulness, I would not say, 'Bhikkhus, cultivate skillfulness.' Since it is possible to cultivate skillfulness, I say, 'Bhikkhus, cultivate skillfulness.' If cultivating skillfulness caused detriment and suffering, I would not say, 'Bhikkhus, cultivate skillfulness.' Since the cultivation of skillfulness brings benefit and happiness, I say, 'Bhikkhus, cultivate skillfulness.'"[65]

And in case you ever get lost on the path, the *Dhammapada* contains one little stanza that sums things up quite nicely: avoid doing bad, cultivate good, and purify your mind.[66]

CHAPTER 13

Skillfulness at the Six Sense Doors

IN THE PRACTICE of Dhamma, the five sense organs, their objects and interactions, plus the mind and its thoughts and interactions are collectively referred to as "the six sense spheres" (*salayatana*). The Buddha made many valuable recommendations on how to meditate with respect to these gates or doors at which consciousness can arise:

> "And how, bhikkhus, does one dwell diligently? If one dwells with restraint over the eye faculty, the mind is not soiled among forms cognizable by the eye. If the mind is not soiled, gladness is born. When one is gladdened, rapture is born. When the mind is uplifted by rapture, the body becomes tranquil. One tranquil in body experiences happiness. The mind of one who is happy becomes concentrated. When the mind is concentrated, phenomena become manifest. Because phenomena become manifest, one is reckoned as one who dwells diligently.
>
> If one dwells with restraint over the ear faculty the mind is not soiled among sounds cognizable by the ear.... If one dwells with restraint over the mind faculty, the mind is not soiled among mental phenomena cognizable by the mind.... Because phenomena become manifest, one is reckoned as one who dwells diligently."[67]

When we develop mindfulness exceptionally well, we experience the deepest level of impermanence in what we see, hear, smell, taste, touch, and become conscious of. The Buddha gave six similes to make this point very clear. Suppose you see an object. It will be instantly pleasant, unpleasant, or neither-pleasant-nor-unpleasant. This initial, almost physiological reaction is so ephemeral that it passes away much faster than lightning. The simile the Buddha likened to this ephemeral nature of feeling sensation is of opening and closing your eyes. Suppose there is an object in front of you. You open your eyes and immediately close them. It might take only a moment for you to open and close your eyes, and during that quick moment you do not have time to form an opinion or feel pleasantness or unpleasantness in relation to the object. There is barely time for neither-pleasant-nor unpleasant feeling. This simile and five others are given in the *Indriyabhavana Sutta, The Discourse on the Development of the Faculties*:

> Just as a man with good sight, having opened his eyes might shut them or having shut his eyes might open them . . . Just as a strong man might easily snap his fingers . . . Just as raindrops on a slightly sloping lotus leaf roll off and do not remain there . . . Just as a strong man might easily spit out a ball of spittle collected on the tip of his tongue . . . Just as a strong man might extend his flexed arm or flex his extended arm, so too . . . Just as if a man were to let two or three drops of water fall onto an iron plate heated for a whole day, the falling of the drops might be slow but they would quickly vaporize and vanish, so too concerning anything at all, the agreeable that arose, the disagreeable that arose, and the both agreeable and disagreeable that arose cease just as quickly, just as rapidly, just as easily, and equanimity is established.[68]

In this discourse the Buddha points out that mindful meditators encounter sights, sounds, smells, tastes, touches, and mind-objects in the same way as do non-meditators. Non-meditators also experience pleasant, unpleasant, and neutral feelings, and they too become delighted, disappointed, or neither. Sometimes the almost immediate neither-pleasant-nor-unpleasant response to thoughts or sensory stimuli is included as one of the types of equanimity described by the Buddha. The difference is that for careful meditators, all of these feeling responses tend to evaporate on arising. Thus meditators of this caliber often dwell peacefully.

Setting Up Your Mindfulness

You too can set up the conditions for careful meditation and peaceful dwelling. Some sources say that you should go to the forest, leave behind conflicts, sit at the root of a tree, or find an empty hut, and then sit in a specific cross-legged fashion, but you can improvise and find what works for you in the modern world. Sit up in a comfortable position. Pay undivided, clean, pure, and quality attention to your every rising and falling breath.

Here we use four words, four technical terms to qualify your attention. *Undivided* means your attention is not divided between the past and future. It should be focused on the breath that rises and falls in the present moment, almost as if your attention were riding on a wave. This is called *parimukham satim* in Pali. *Sati* is mindfulness, and *parimukha* means "in front," in the present moment, in the now. You can notice your breath rising and falling only right now. You cannot notice the rising and falling of past breaths; they are gone. You cannot notice the rising and falling of future breaths; they have yet to occur. You can only see the current moment's breath as it rises and falls right now. "Come and see" this for yourself.

You can practice *clean attention*, in that it is possible to rein in the attention from distracting peripheral stimuli. This is a cooling type of non-interference, what could be called "bare" or "nonreactive attention," yet it is still influenced by conditioning. The popular phrase "guarding the sense doors" means that you can become savvy at restraining the senses, so that each arising sensation or thought is in line with the goal of liberation through wisdom. Phenomena are unfolding and moving, but with momentum the aware mind just glides along smoothly without sticking to any of them.

Pure attention means the attention is without greed, hatred, or confusion in your mind. Pure attention becomes quality attention.

Quality attention includes clear comprehension (*sampajanna*). In classical terms, *sati*, remembrance or mindfulness, is often mentioned together with *sampajanna*. This means that mindfulness of the object of meditation occurs in concert with attentiveness to its larger context. It also implies an unceasing mindfulness throughout every activity and every posture, wherein each transition is fully deliberate and imbued with the continuous experience of impermanence. The canonical commentaries elaborate four further aspects of sampajanna having to do with circumspection and sense restraint: the purpose, domain, suitability, and non-confusion of your participation in each activity. Each of these is discussed below. "Come and see" if you can apply attention that is free from the habits of wanting and not wanting, and if you can sustain this type of attention with every mental and physical activity, in every position of the body, and during every shift from one posture to another.

Purpose

We meditate to purify the mind, to overcome sorrow and lamentation, to overcome grief and despair, to enter the noble eightfold path, and to attain liberation from suffering or dissatisfaction. That is our purpose in quality attention.

Domain

The domain of our meditation practice is fourfold: body, feelings, mind, and mind-objects. These are the spheres in which our quality attention can be maintained without getting pulled elsewhere.

Suitability

We must know that the object we focus our mind upon is suitable for achieving our purpose, as mentioned above, for purifying the mind and so forth.

Non-Confusion

Our quality attention is imbued with clarity and wisdom. It is informed by the three characteristics of impermanence, selflessness, and unsatisfactoriness. It is not personal.

AN EXCELLENT OBJECT

There is a traditional list of meditation objects. Practitioners can choose one that works well for their individual capacities in accordance with all of the qualities above in order to achieve their ultimate aim. One such object that satisfies these criteria quite well, and works nicely for most people, is the breath, which we will focus on here. It is endowed with the factors we find in any conditioned thing. For instance, it can be characterized by rising and falling. The breath arises and the breath falls. It goes in and out through the nose; it causes the rising and falling of the chest and abdominal area. Rising and falling, appearing and disappearing, expanding and contracting are the nature of all conditioned things that exist in the universe. The breath exemplifies this reality.

As we pay attention to the rising and falling of the breath, we notice the contact of the breath with the nose; feelings (sensations) that are pleasant, unpleasant, or neither will arise and pass away. Feelings depend upon this contact. We perceive all of this and become aware of whatever thoughts and consciousnesses rise and fall. When we keep paying nonverbal attention to these risings and fallings, our body, our breathing, and our mind become calm and relaxed.

At this stage, greed or covetousness, the first of the five hindrances, fades away. Desire cannot hold on to anything that is always in motion, rising and falling, appearing and disappearing. And so our minds become calmer and more relaxed. In this relaxed state of mind any rigidity, uptightness, or resentment, the second hindrance, fades away. Therefore the mind relaxes further still and grows peaceful. This is the state where we begin to feel metta.

When breath, body, and mind are calm and relaxed, and we experience the feeling of metta, there is a kind of synchrony that occurs. Continuing to focus the mind on the breath while imbued with metta, we might become so calm and peaceful that sometimes we fall asleep. Sleep is very sweet. We do not have to wish for it. We automatically feel its sweetness. We want to welcome it and embrace it with both hands. However, when we wake up from sleep, we do not necessarily wake up with new insight. Instead we actually become duller after sleeping. This hindrance is sometimes called "sloth and torpor." The longer we sleep, the duller we become. Therefore if and when this happens, we must rouse energy to overcome sleepiness. We must galvanize the attention in service of our goal.

We can remind ourselves that finding a moment to be calm and meditate is very rare in this life. Despite our daily commitments and obligations, we have found that precious opportunity, so we should not be so foolish as to let it slip away. We sleep every day, but most of us do not meditate every day. We must use each priceless moment to learn something from meditation to purify our minds, overcome sorrow, lamentation, grief, and despair; to enter the noble eightfold path and attain liberation from suffering.

Once we have overcome sleepiness, our minds can also fall into the opposite: the hindrance of restlessness and worry. In that case we should mindfully apply calming factors of enlightenment such as tranquility, concentration, and equanimity. We must go back to our breath, breathing in and breathing out slowly, paying undivided attention to our breath without letting the mind go to the past or future. We must be wary when it brings up past memories and future plans. Stay in the present moment.

Continue paying non-verbal attention to the breath until restlessness and worry fade away.

Having taken care of these hindrances, we continue paying attention to the breath. At this point it is possible that doubt might arise in the mind. Perhaps we question our potential for success in achieving the aim of meditation. We may ask, "Can I accomplish anything at all?" We might wonder if we are doing it right, thinking, "My legs are hurting. My body is hurting. I do not know if I am doing this correctly. Is there another way?" We might question the person, place, or time: "Are these instructions correct? Should I seek another teacher? Maybe this is not the right meditation environment for me." When the hindrance of doubt arises, it can come up with all sorts of uncertainties. Just notice the doubt.

First, you should reflect on your own recent success so far in overcoming four out of five hindrances—greed, hatred, sleepiness, and restlessness and worry. This arouses confidence in your ability. Next, think of the Buddha, who practiced all of this. The Buddha was a real person who achieved all of the above-named purposes and much more in his lifetime, not to mention teaching the Dhamma for decades. Thinking like this generates assuredness in your mind. Many thousands of people have practiced this time-tested method and realized the aims of mindfulness meditation. I have seen that even some of my hindrances are gone. I am sure that I will attain some of the purposes of this meditation. I am sure that with right practice you can, too.

What About Concentration?

With full confidence you pay attention to your breath. You immerse yourself in it. Your body and mind are calmer now, more relaxed and peaceful. You are happy that you have overcome the five hindrances.

Greed is allayed. Having a greedy mind is like using borrowed goods and money. Living with desire is like living with all kinds of debts to pay, but overcoming desire is like getting rid of those debts. Suppose you are wearing a borrowed expensive outfit for somebody's wedding party. You are walking proudly here and there in the crowd, rubbing shoulders and feeling popular, until the person who loaned you the fancy outfit comes up and taps you on the shoulder, saying, "I have promised to loan this outfit to another customer tomorrow morning. Make sure you return it as soon as the party is over." Even though you are annoyed about returning the expensive outfit, you feel great relief once you do. Similarly, when you have overcome the hindrance of greed, you feel relief, happiness.

Anger is allayed. Anger is like sickness, and living without anger is like being free from sickness. When you are sick you cannot taste food no matter how tasty it is, you do not enjoy anything, and you do not like anybody. When you recover from your sickness you taste food, you enjoy everything, and you like everybody. Then you are happy. Similarly, when your anger disappears you are happy.

Lethargy is allayed. Being sleepy or drowsy is like being in a maximum-security prison cell. You are confined to four walls, a floor, and a ceiling, and freeing yourself from sleepiness and drowsiness is like coming out of jail. When you are released from the prison cell, you are free to go anywhere and do anything you like, and you are happy.

Agitation is allayed. Having restlessness and worry is like being enslaved. When you are a slave to anybody or anything, you feel trapped and restless. Suppose you are a slave to your own unwholesome habits—gambling or drinking, alcohol or sex. You will always be restless in such a state. But once you overcome these habits, you are more at ease. Similarly, when you overcome restlessness and worry, you are happy.

Doubt is allayed. This type of hesitation and anxiety is like a desert without roads, road signs, or directions of any sort. There is neither food nor water, and there are no fellow human beings. You are alone, at a loss of where to go. But having found your way out somehow and emerged from the desert, you are glad.

Similarly, when you are free from greed, hatred, sleepiness and drowsiness, restlessness and worry, and doubt, you are happy. One who is happy gains concentration.

When a mind that is mindful and meditating unites with the rising and falling, inhaling and exhaling breath, this state is called *samma samadhi*, "right concentration." This is a clear state allowing for deep awareness of impermanence. In such a state you perceive the impermanence of the breath as well as that of the feeling tones that arise dependent on contact with the breath. You perceive the impermanence of perceptions, thoughts, and consciousness. Your domain is the field of the fourfold establishment of mindfulness (*satipatthana gocara*). Your resort is also right thought (*samma samkappa gocara*), such as thoughts of renunciation (*nekkhamma samkappa*), thoughts of loving-friendliness (*avyapada samkappa*, literally "without ill will"), and thoughts of compassion (*avihimsa samkappa*, literally "merciful" or "without cruelty"). The mind is gathered and collected here, free from distraction. It shines brightly, and things seem clear. That is why the Buddha said the concentrated mind sees things as they really are.

When people who are not mindful see impermanence over and over again, they get bored and tired. But if you truly practice mindfulness, then looking at impermanence again and again is interesting. Eventually your wisdom eye will open to profound acuity. This is hardly a dull experience. You will see more deeply than with regular eyes, with greater precision to penetrate the more subtle changes in your body, feelings, perceptions, thoughts, and consciousness. You will see that all these aggregates are changing every fraction of a second. You will be happy that the same truth prevails in everything and glad that you did not give up in your effort to "come and see." Now you have a powerful tool for the breakthrough to lasting peace.

The Lion and the Dog

When you gain concentration, you see things as they are (*samahito cittam yathabhutam pajanati*).[69] You become clearly aware of the breath; the contact of the breath; the feeling tones that arise depending on that contact; and perceptions, thoughts, and consciousness. These are the five aggregates, and now you can see them for what they are: collections of things. Breath is a collection of tiny, little particles of air containing oxygen atoms. Feeling is a collection of many kinds of feelings—pleasant, unpleasant, neutral, carnal, non-carnal, deep, shallow, gross, or subtle—arising through eye-contact, ear-contact, nose-contact, tongue-contact, body-contact, and mind-contact. Perception is a collection of perceptions of forms, sounds, smells, tastes, touches, and mind-objects. Fabrication is a collection of fabrications—thoughts of forms, sounds, smells, tastes, touches, and mind-objects. Similarly for emotions. The consciousness aggregate is a collection of many states of consciousness: eye-consciousness, ear-consciousness, nose-consciousness, tongue-consciousness, body-consciousness, and mind-consciousness.

Remaining fully aware, we can know what happens to these aggregates, too. We can see them becoming and transforming instantaneously in every moment as we breathe in and breathe out. To see this reality we must learn to go all the way to the root of their arising. We can follow the breath to that root of becoming. When we breathe in mindfully, we become aware of each breath and notice the touch of the breath somewhere—at the nostrils, the tip of the nose, the upper lips, or the expansion of our lungs as they fill with the breath, perhaps expanding our lower abdomen. When we breathe out, we notice the breath leaving while touching the same places and disappearing. These functions are taking place continuously as we breathe in and out.

If the mind wanders here and there, we must be more mindful. In Pali this is called *yoniso manasikara*, which can be translated into English as "attend to the root." We must always learn to go to the root (*yoni*). The Buddha gave a meaningful simile regarding this starting place for all that is. If you throw a stick or rock, a dog would likely run after it. That dog would either bite it or bring it back to you. A lion would not run after the stick or the rock. He or she would run after you instead! The lion goes to the root, while the dog runs away from it. Unmindful people go after sensory objects and get bewildered. Those who are mindful, on the other hand, want to find the root of the entire process.

If we breathe mindfully, we can notice all five of the aggregates changing or rising and falling so rapidly that we cannot keep up with them, and yet we are aware of each of them rising and falling. Particles of air that we breathe in and out are participating in this rise and fall. Contacts rise and fall. Feelings, perceptions, thoughts, and consciousnesses rise and fall. We must remain like lions, not like dogs. Then we can "come and see" the meaning of those six similes from the *Indriyabhavana Sutta*.

The lion does not let the prey escape. Similarly, we use our mindfulness to overcome the fetters and hindrances so that the object of our practice comes into focus. As the Buddha said so insightfully in the *Aniccasanna Sutta, The Discourse on the Perception of Impermanence*, when we use our mindfulness to really see the rising and falling of all ten armies of Mara, we experience each of them falling one by one. We see every adversary disappearing in the face of mindfulness.[70]

CHAPTER 14

"Come and See" Is Not "Come and Believe"

SINCE WE MUST look at the mind with sincerity in order to see its inner workings, the Buddha taught with a spirit of free self-assessment. When the Kalama people in ancient India requested his advice about the various doctrines and teachers of their time, he recommended that they trust themselves first and foremost. In a radical departure from the popular and raucous debates between proponents of certain ideologies, he did not necessarily chastise those with views different from his own. In the *Kalama Sutta* he merely said to not trust any belief without proper investigation, advising the Kalamas to test internally for themselves whether or not a teaching would indeed lead to wholesome results in the heart and mind:

> "Come, Kālāmas, do not go by oral tradition, by lineage of teaching, by hearsay, by a collection of scriptures, by logical reasoning, by inferential reasoning, by reasoned cogitation, by the acceptance of a view after pondering it, by the seeming competence [of a speaker], or because you think: 'The ascetic is our guru.' But when, Kālāmas, you know for yourselves: 'These things are unwholesome; these things are blameworthy; these things are censured by the wise; these things, if accepted and undertaken, lead to harm and suffering,' then you should abandon them."

The Buddha then helps the Kalama people investigate greed, hatred, and delusion, one by one, so that they can see for themselves that each is unwholesome. Then they reflect, one by one, on the wholesome traits of non-greed, non-hatred, and non-delusion.

> "What do you think, Kālāmas? Are these things wholesome or unwholesome?" – "Wholesome, Bhante." – "Blameworthy or blameless?" – "Blameless, Bhante." – "Censured or praised by the wise?" – "Praised by the wise, Bhante." – "Accepted and undertaken, do they lead to welfare and happiness or not, or how do you take it?" – "Accepted and undertaken, these things lead to welfare and happiness. So [personally discerning thus,] we take it."
>
> "Thus, Kālāmas, when we said: 'Come, Kālāmas, do not go by oral tradition . . . But when you know for yourselves: 'These things are wholesome; these things are blameless; these things are praised by the wise; these things, if accepted and undertaken, lead to welfare and happiness,' then you should live in accordance with them.'"

Do not be fooled into believing that the Buddha's only goal was to get the Kalamas to think for themselves, or even to distinguish between wholesome and unwholesome in pursuit of worldly happiness. He then described how abiding by what one knows for oneself can lead to immeasurable good tidings:

> Then, Kālāmas, that noble disciple, who is thus devoid of longing, devoid of ill will, unconfused, clearly comprehending, ever mindful, dwells pervading one quarter with a mind imbued with loving-kindness . . . with a mind imbued with compassion . . . with a mind imbued with altruistic joy . . . with a mind imbued with equanimity, likewise the second quarter,

the third quarter, and the fourth quarter. Thus above, below, across, and everywhere, and to all as to himself, he dwells pervading the entire world with a mind imbued with equanimity, vast, exalted, measureless, without enmity, without ill will.

Then, after showing how trusting in the depth of our own personal experience can lead us quite naturally to dwell in the classic four divine abidings, the Buddha recounted four broader ways in which it is possible to rest assured in choosing wholesomeness.

> "This noble disciple, Kālāmas, whose mind is in this way without enmity, without ill will, undefiled, and pure, has won four assurances in this very life.
>
> The first assurance he has won is this: 'If there is another world, and if there is the fruit and result of good and bad deeds, it is possible that with the breakup of the body, after death, I will be reborn in a good destination, in a heavenly world.'
>
> "The second assurance he has won is this: 'If there is no other world, and there is no fruit and result of good and bad deeds, still right here, in this very life, I maintain myself in happiness, without enmity and ill will, free of trouble.'
>
> "The third assurance he has won is this: "Suppose evil comes to one who does evil. Then, when I have no evil intentions toward anyone, how can suffering afflict me, since I do no evil deed?'
>
> "The fourth assurance he has won is this: 'Suppose evil does not come to one who does evil. Then right here I see myself purified in both respects.'
>
> "This noble disciple, Kālāmas, whose mind is in this way without enmity, without ill will, undefiled, and pure, has won these four assurances in this very life."[71]

Although his concluding words to the Kalama people are often obscured by the popularity of the Buddha's remarks about reasonable inquiry, the four solaces, as these reassurances are sometimes called, help us to see that living a good life in the present is a failsafe approach to happiness that is independent of belief in future rebirth. We can "come and see" for ourselves that freedom from greed, hatred, and delusion is worth it in the here and now.

CRITERION OF JUDGMENT

Is this spirit of free thought so generous that anything goes? The Buddha tells the monks of the four *mahapadesas* that they should respect. *Maha* means "great, big" or "important," while *padesa* refers to an indicator of regional boundary, in this case the extent to which a teaching can be incorporated into one's way of life. If a monk says that he has received "a certain teaching directly from the Buddha himself, then his statement should be compared with the rest of the Vinaya (the discipline) and Dhamma (the doctrine)."[72] If these, the code of conduct and the teachings, do not agree with that monk's statement, then the newly recounted version is to be rejected. If they do accord, then the custom dictates that the statement should be accepted.

The same guiding principle applies to whatever is said to have been learned from a group of monastics led by a *theri* or *thera*, elders in our tradition. Likewise for teachings heard from a body of senior monks residing in a certain place, or from a single senior monk proficient in the Dhamma, the Vinaya, and the *matika*.[73]

When we "come and see" on any of these levels, whether the instructive stories of Dhamma, the Vinaya code of conduct, or the highly refined codification of experience as outlined in the matika; when we look within without prejudice, we see if there is any conflict between our personal realization and the original teachings of the Buddha. In that way we have a method for how to recognize and correct subjective bias.

The Buddha's teaching is consistent. If there is any inconsistency, then it is most likely not the Buddha's teaching. To know what the Buddha did and did not teach, there is a simple test. We must ask, "Does this agree with the four noble truths or not?" If the teaching heard does not agree directly or indirectly with these four indisputable aspects of being human, if it is not in alignment with them, then it is not the Buddha's teaching.

There is suffering. There is a cause for suffering, and the cause is craving. There is an end to suffering, and it is possible to experience that end. We can cultivate and develop that path leading to the end of suffering.

The Buddha's Solution to Fear and Sorrow

With the attitude of "come and see," we can be brave. Informed by the experience of impermanence, we can look right into difficulty while knowing that everything arises from causes and conditions. We know that it is not worth the pain of holding tightly on to something or someone, or even to a sense of self, when the supporting causes and conditions for these things are always changing. Guided by this penetrating insight into nature as it is, we become curious about real situations that we used to pretend would go away.

When we acknowledge death as a part of life, for instance, we can have more spaciousness around habitual physiological responses that protect the body. Consider the way our hearts race when we realize we've nearly stepped on a snake. The programming for any breathing being to protect its life is deep. A living being that relies upon only the reptilian brain will either fight with or flee from fierce animals. We humans have a sizeable neocortex, and if we remain present with a well-tuned heart, we can practice to increase our options.

The Buddha advised us to avoid these ferocious creatures altogether so that we do not have to fight or flee. These two types of reactions are caused by our fear in service of protecting life. Whether we fight or flee, we cannot stop death. Sooner or later it comes. Those fierce animals and us—we all meet at one point. That intersection is our death.

Fierce animals attack us out of fear. We attack them out of fear. With that fear, both we and they fight or run away. There is no difference between them and us in this regard. The Buddha's advice is that we ought to understand the nature of beings, whether human or non-human, and respect one another. When we respect the lives of ferocious beings and keep them at a distance, they go their ways respecting us. This is how compassion arises spontaneously from the wisdom of how things are.

All unenlightened beings are attached to their lives. Craving generates fear for the maintenance of life and also sorrow when we are about to lose that personal sense of being alive. With the destruction of desire, the Dhamma protects us from both fear and sorrow, and they disappear.

CHAPTER 15

Impermanence in Every Breath

RIGHT CONCENTRATION

WHAT IS right concentration? A number of ascetic sects in ancient India advocated techniques to concentrate the mind, yet they were varied enough that the Kalama people wondered whose practice to trust. The four noble truths as set forth by the Buddha assert that there is a way leading to liberation from suffering and that such a way can be cultivated. Right concentration, since it is part of that eightfold path to be cultivated, must therefore function to lead us toward the goal of liberation. In Buddhist meditation we develop serenity insofar as it conduces to wisdom, because wisdom is what liberates. Toward this end, concentration that generates wisdom generally involves a collected state of wholesome consciousness. To be precise, this concentration occurs in concert with right thinking, right effort, and right mindfulness.

In meditation we develop mindfulness, which is seeing things as they are. When practiced with concentration, it leads to insight. Insight opens to wisdom. The *Atthakanagara Sutta*,[74] *The Discourse to the Man from Atthaka*, mentions that even when you are in the first of the deeply absorbed concentration states, or jhanas, you can develop mindfulness and concentration together to see things as they really are.

If you practice concentration without mindfulness, then you will need to come out of jhana before you can add the practice of mindfulness. But if you start out with right concentration, which includes mindfulness from the very beginning, then you do not have to come out of concentration in order to practice mindfulness to see things as they really are. This must be clear in your mind. You have to know whether there is concentration with mindfulness or not.

You should ensure that your concentration flows continuously, with full awareness of the rising and falling of sights, sounds, smells, tastes, touches, and thoughts that you have had through your eyes, ears, nose, tongue, body, and mind. Then, while paying total attention to your breathing, you feel your breath. You notice your perception of the breath, feeling the rising and falling of both the feeling and the breath, even as they are changing. You notice your thoughts and consciousness. They too rise and fall. Breaths, feelings, perceptions, thoughts, and consciousness are not there as you might have believed. They arise and pass away. Remember that what passes away is that which arose. You do not find anything fixed or static. Whatever arises passes away. This is the nature of impermanence.

When you begin your concentration with mindfulness from the outset, you can go all the way to the attainment of total freedom. You stay mindful of impermanence. Even when you attain the cessation of perception and feelings, you see impermanence. When you stay with mindfulness, you can see many mental factors rising and falling. None of them is actually there in a discrete sort of way; rather, they arise and pass away just like bubbles in a pond when it rains. Bubbles are not inherently in the pond. Only when it rains and drops of water fall onto the water can bubbles appear and disappear. Whatever appears disappears.

Seeing the Venerable Sariputta in meditation, the Buddha described the mental states of that monk whose practice had led to great wisdom and joy, saying:

> "And the states in the first jhāna—the applied thought, the sustained thought, the rapture, the pleasure, and the unifi-
> cation of mind . . . And the states in the second jhāna—the
> self-confidence, the rapture, the pleasure, and the unification

of mind . . . And the states in the third jhāna—the equanimity, the pleasure, the mindfulness, the full awareness, and the unification of mind . . . And the states in the fourth jhāna—the equanimity, the neither-painful-nor-pleasant feeling, the mental unconcern due to tranquility, the purity of mindfulness, and the unification of mind; the contact, feeling, perception, volition, and mind; the zeal, decision, energy, mindfulness, equanimity, and attention—these states were defined by him one by one as they occurred, known to him those states arose, known they were present, known they disappeared. He understood thus: 'So indeed, these states, not having been, come into being; having been, they vanish.'"

After describing the jhanic concentrations of the form realms, the Buddha articulated the conditions for entering more distilled formless realms or immaterial jhana states:

"And the states in the base of infinite space—the perception of the base of infinite space and the unification of mind . . . And the states in the base of infinite consciousness—the perception of the base of infinite consciousness and the unification of mind . . . And the states in the base of nothingness—the perception of the base of nothingness and the unification of mind . . . He understood thus: 'So indeed, these states, not having been, come into being; having been, they vanish.'"[75]

Let us see what appears and disappears when you enter the jhanas. As your concentration grows stronger and stronger, the number of thoughts will diminish. Sometimes you will notice "initial thought" (*sankappa*). Initial thought is the purpose and intention of the thinking, whereas "applied thought" (*vitakka*) is the inception of the thought itself. Initial thoughts might include thoughts of renunciation (*nekkhamma sankappa*), thoughts of non-hatred or metta (*avyapada sankappa*), and thoughts of compassion, non-cruelty, or not hurting any being in the world (*avihimsa sankappa*).

At times confidence arises in the Buddha, the Dhamma, the Sangha, and in yourself. Between these moments of assurance your mind might go to memories of past sights and sounds. You may see the impermanence of them all. Or you may remember the image of the Buddha. Sometimes you will remember entire sequences of events. Sometimes, things seem to occur randomly. You might remember lists of things that you studied earlier. Suddenly you realize that you have drifted away from your main practice. This is the nature of everyone's mind. All of these, even drifting away from your main practice, are examples of rising and falling.

Drifting away. Thoughts. Concentration rising and falling. Then you recall the first instruction: "the applied thought, the sustained thought, the rapture, the pleasure, and the unification of mind." You recall the second instruction: "the self-confidence, the rapture, the pleasure, and the unification of mind." You proceed up to the fourth instruction: "the equanimity, the neither-painful-nor-pleasant feeling, the mental uncon-cern due to tranquility, the purity of mindfulness, and the unification of mind; the contact, feeling, perception, volition, and mind."[76] And from here, you are ready to explore further refinement.

The first sutta mentioned in this chapter, the *Atthakanagara Sutta*, actually covers eleven ways to escape the fires of stress. They include the four jhana states in the form realm plus the brahma viharas, but only the first three of the formless jhanas. After that, when you attain the "base of neither-perception-nor-non-perception" you do not notice any mental state *per se*; the mental factors involved here are too subtle for the aim of the discourse. When you emerge from that state, you can enter upon and abide in the "cessation of perception and feeling." This is the most refined temporary state of concentration to be formally described in my tradi-tion. By looking with the resultant degree of clarity and wisdom, you can see how any grasping at all leads to stress. Thus, while inclining your mind toward true cessation as your mental object, you can end what are called the "taints of experience" with this method.

Develop All the Factors of Awakening

Seeing things as they are, you can develop all the factors of awakening (*sambojjhanga*). These wholesome factors that support awakening are mindfulness, investigation, energy, joy, tranquility, concentration, and equanimity. Additionally there are seven sets of qualities (*bodhipakkhiyadhamma*) that the Buddha was said to exemplify. You can gain continuity of insight into impermanence, non-self, and the transformation of suffering by cultivating these sets of awakened qualities:

> The view of a person such as this is right view. His intention is right intention, his effort is right effort, his mindfulness is right mindfulness, his concentration is right concentration. But his bodily action, his verbal action, and his livelihood have already been well purified earlier. Thus this Noble Eightfold Path comes to fulfilment in him by development. When he develops this Noble Eightfold Path, the four foundations of mindfulness . . . the four right kinds of striving . . . the four bases for spiritual power . . . the five faculties . . . the five powers . . . the seven enlightenment factors also come to fulfilment in him by development. These two things—serenity and insight—occur in him yoked evenly together. He fully understands by direct knowledge those things that should be fully understood by direct knowledge. He abandons by direct knowledge those things that should be abandoned by direct knowledge. He develops by direct knowledge those things that should be developed by direct knowledge. He realises by direct knowledge those things that should be realised by direct knowledge.

And what things should be fully understood by direct knowledge? The answer to that is: the five aggregates affected by clinging, that is, the material form aggregate . . . the feeling aggregate . . . the perception aggregate . . . the formations aggregate . . . the consciousness aggregate affected by clinging. These are the things that should be fully understood by direct knowledge.

And what things should be abandoned by direct knowledge? Ignorance and craving for being. These are the things that should be abandoned by direct knowledge.

And what things should be developed by direct knowledge? Serenity and insight. These are the things that should be developed by direct knowledge.

And what things should be realised by direct knowledge? True knowledge and deliverance. These are the things that should be realised by direct knowledge.[77]

Now you have many tools for practice. If you generate these qualities, they will give rise to greater freedom, and you will see your mind becoming calmer, more peaceful, as the defilements wane. Nobody but you can become fully aware of this personal experience as you approach liberation from suffering. You will recognize the aforementioned direct knowledge with honesty and sincerity. This knowing is neither flashy nor hypocritical, but genuine and quiet. There will be no doubt whatsoever in the validity of your experience.

SEEING IS BELIEVING

What informs this authentic seeing? Impermanence. Every moment is a changing moment, and therefore you go on changing till midnight. At that point, if you are still awake, you can understand that one second before was yesterday and the next second after that became today.

One second earlier, that next second would have been tomorrow. Time changes so quickly that today disappears at the speed of blinking my eyes. My personal life in the present moment is limited to less than one second. Just like yours. You can experience this yourself. You do not need to learn it from any external source—parents, teachers, friends, relatives, or anybody or anything other than your concentrated mind. This is why the Buddha said that a "concentrated mind sees things as they are."[78]

Seeing with your eyes may or may not reveal what is true. Often you hear people say, "Seeing is believing." The Buddha might not have used these exact words, but he knew and taught how to see things as they are. Seeing, hearing, smelling, and touching can be distorted by numerous factors. But if you maintain your mindfulness, your deeply concentrated mind can see directly while remaining free from distortion. In this way you can see material as well as non-physical changes.

Physicists can see most material things with the aid of their physical eyes, often in combination with powerful microscopes and telescopes. Your concentrated and mindful mind can see how anything that comes into existence is also going out of existence. This anything can be material or immaterial, far or near, gross or subtle, internal or external. All you need is physical seclusion, mental seclusion, and the powerful combination of mindfulness plus concentration. Seclusion from unnecessary or unwholesome input creates a space for you to enjoy freedom from various defilements; it helps you to foster a mind that is pure, clean, and unhindered. Then the excellent pairing of mindfulness and concentration not only sharpens your mind but also facilitates the arising of wisdom so that you can look at what you experience without bias or aberration.

Some people cannot see impermanence so clearly when just beginning to practice; they need training. In all likelihood this is why the Buddha mentioned impermanence at the end rather than at the beginning of the *Anapanasati Sutta, The Discourse on Mindfulness of Breathing.* As their proficiency in meditation increases, trainees develop their facilities of mindfulness and concentration. Then they too will begin to see impermanence more clearly. And at the culmination of this endeavor they will see nothing but the rising and falling, or the appearing and disappearing, of the breath. As in the story of Bahiya Daruciriya, some people see impermanence right away; however, even for those who initially struggle, once mindfulness and concentration are well developed it is easy to see impermanence.

Consider the range of capacities shown by eight monks who told the Buddha how they meditated on death:

> (1) [...] "Here, Bhante, I think thus: 'May I live just a night and a day so that I may attend to the Blessed One's teaching. I could then accomplish much!' It is in this way that I develop mindfulness of death."
>
> (2) Another bhikkhu said to the Blessed One: "I too, Bhante, develop mindfulness of death. [...] Here, Bhante, I think: 'May I live just a day so that I may attend to the Blessed One's teaching. I could then accomplish much!' It is in this way that I develop mindfulness of death."
>
> (3) Still another bhikkhu said to the Blessed One: "I too, Bhante, develop mindfulness of death. [...] Here, Bhante, I think: 'May I live just half a day so that I may attend to the Blessed One's teaching. I could then accomplish much!' It is in this way that I develop mindfulness of death."
>
> (4) Still another bhikkhu said to the Blessed One: "I too, Bhante, develop mindfulness of death. [...] Here, Bhante, I think: 'May I live just the time it takes to eat a single alms meal so that I may attend to the Blessed One's teaching. I could then accomplish much!' It is in this way that I develop mindfulness of death."
>
> (5) Still another bhikkhu said to the Blessed One: "I too, Bhante, develop mindfulness of death. [...] Here, Bhante, I think: 'May I live just the time it takes to eat half an alms meal

so that I may attend to the Blessed One's teaching. I could then accomplish much!' It is in this way that I develop mindfulness of death."

(6) Still another bhikkhu said to the Blessed One: "I too, Bhante, develop mindfulness of death. [...] Here, Bhante, I think: 'May I live just the time it takes to chew and swallow four or five mouthfuls of food so that I may attend to the Blessed One's teaching. I could then accomplish much!' It is in this way that I develop mindfulness of death."

(7) Still another bhikkhu said to the Blessed One: "I too, Bhante, develop mindfulness of death. [...] Here, Bhante, I think: 'May I live just the time it takes to chew and swallow a single mouthful of food so that I may attend to the Blessed One's teaching. I could then accomplish much!' It is in this way that I develop mindfulness of death."

(8) Still another bhikkhu said to the Blessed One: "I too, Bhante, develop mindfulness of death. [...] Here, Bhante, I think: 'May I live just the time it takes to breathe out after breathing in, or to breathe in after breathing out, so that I may attend to the Blessed One's teaching. I could then accomplish much!' It is in this way that I develop mindfulness of death."

After listening to all of them, the Buddha praised the seventh and eighth monks, saying that they dwelled heedfully and developed mindfulness of impermanence more clearly than the other six monks. Those six monks were living heedlessly, he said, and practiced mindfulness of death sluggishly, while the last two developed "mindfulness of death keenly for the destruction of the taints."[79]

An object of mind like death reminds us of its inevitability and rouses our sense of urgency. Those who refine concentration and mindfulness with this intensity and diligence can inspire us. Impermanence is immanent, and by attuning the mind in a certain way we can generate awareness of specific aspects of the mind, leading to peace. Take, for instance, the *Mindfulness of Breathing Discourse*:

> He trains thus: "I shall breathe in contemplating imperma-
> nence"; he trains thus: "I shall breathe out contemplating
> impermanence." He trains thus: "I shall breathe in contem-
> plating fading away"; he trains thus: "I shall breathe out con-
> templating fading away." He trains thus: "I shall breathe in
> contemplating cessation"; he trains thus: "I shall breathe out
> contemplating cessation." He trains thus: "I shall breathe
> in contemplating relinquishment"; he trains thus: "I shall
> breathe out contemplating relinquishment."[80]

Without saying "impermanence of" something, the discourse simply mentions "contemplating impermanence." With a well-trained mind, impermanence can remain a salient feature of our experience even as specific sensory objects like the breath drop away.

HAPPENINGS IN MOTION

We are each a moving collection of activities. In every moment something or other is happening in us. We read or walk, talk or write. While we move here and there during these activities, countless things are happening. Our hearts keep beating. They are busily receiving deoxygenated blood from all over the body, sending it to the lungs for oxygen and then pumping that oxygen-rich blood to all of the tissues and organs. The lungs are also busy receiving deoxygenated blood from the heart, charging the blood with the oxygen that they breathe in and then sending it back to the heart. Veins and arteries are constantly carrying blood and nutrients to each tiny cell while also collecting the oxygen-depleted blood and waste for transport.

The liver is metabolizing; the kidneys are filtering and excreting; every kind of cell must function properly without delay. They all are very busy. Nothing in our bodies remains idle. Nothing has time to rest. Even during sleep, so many parts of our bodies are working to keep us alive, not to mention the thoughts and feelings, sensations and emotions, endlessly informing our notions of self. All of the time all of these processes are in motion. Therefore we need not look for one specific part of ourselves to see impermanence. Likewise we do not need to travel to some special place. All we must do to realize impermanence is pay attention to what is really going on inside this very body and mind. By showing up, by merely participating with this inner looking, we "come and see." It takes only a moment of direct mindfulness with just enough concentration; it could be at the stroke of midnight or while eating a single morsel of food. This is why the Buddha said, "All dhammas arise from attention" (*Manasikara sambhava sabbe dhamma*).[81] "Come and see" mindfully. We can see impermanence in every breath. The eighth monk was so heedful that one breath was enough for him to attain liberation. You might not have to be a monk. This is an open invitation. Ehipassiko.

Why Impermanence Meditation?

I F THE TASTE of impermanence offered in this book has not yet compelled your further practice, here are two very real reasons to engage in impermanence meditation within this lifetime: death and nibbana. Everybody is familiar with the idea of impermanence; we might even think we know that we are born, grow old, and pass away. But mere awareness of this eventuality is not enough.

Whether you are a ninety-five-year-old monk or an athlete in the prime of your life, you must understand that you can die at any moment, by heart attack, stroke, brain dysfunction, kidney failure, accident, or snake bite, and that any of these can happen while you are sleeping, walking, talking, or lying down—at any moment. If your goal in meditation is freedom, you do not want the moment of death to occur when your mind is occupied with greed, hatred, delusion, or any of their associates. Death is with you during each instant of aliveness, so you must do your best to keep the mind continuously pure, clean, and free from worry, tension, anxiety, anger, hatred, and jealousy. Through insight wisdom, you can clear the mind of all such difficulties and distractions, so that at death, your opportunity for freedom will not be waylaid by unwholesome mental qualities. The sooner you relinquish them, the better.

If your purpose is peace, then the fearless acknowledgment of death and impermanence helps you to generate the most appropriate motivation to achieve that aim. What is the motivation that leads to peace? You should have the intention to live the rest of your life without the three poisons of greed, hatred, and delusion polluting your mind. This will make for a more peaceful life and also foster conditions for a death that is less mentally painful, agonizing, confusing, and worrisome. For this reason, I always meditate on impermanence. And every time anger arises in me, I release it. If I remember something hurtful that someone has done to me, I immediately switch my mind to mindfulness of impermanence and eliminate whatever resentment arises in the mind. I try to keep the mind very pure and clean all the time.

Perhaps you have seen elderly people who are easily agitated or irritated. Their bodies are breaking down and they cannot do what they used to be able to do. When I was younger, people did not want to walk with me because I was too fast for them, but now, nobody wants to walk with me because I am too slow. Remembering the capacities and capabilities of their youth, sometimes older people get upset. I do not get upset, nor do I become agitated. Insight, maturity, and wisdom are far more pleasing than clinging to anything that depends upon changing circumstances.

When you practice mindfulness of impermanence, keep your mind pure and clean, knowing that you can die at any moment. Recollect your intent for that very instant of ending to be without greed, hatred, or delusion. The mental continuum is one aspect of the dying process where you do have an effect. When you live each day in the light of your own mortality, you are aware that the experience of your "self" is not static. You can remind yourself that anything impermanent is necessarily empty of a truly independent self (*sunnata*). This nonexistence of a concrete self, along with signlessness (*animitta*, the absence of fixed notions of what is and what is not) and aimlessness (*appanihita*, the absence of the longing to satisfy craving), are openings to the liberated heart. You can set your course toward freedom accordingly. Of course, there is really nowhere to go.

It is said that when we breathe our very last breath, various signs can appear in the final mind-moment. What happens next depends upon which of these is ready to propel us forward. Sometimes, a very strong action (*kamma*) committed in this life, whether wholesome or unwholesome, will appear as a memory and drive the experience of our passing. Cause and effect need not be deep or esoteric. If the person dying did not perform any seriously heavy act during the course of their lifetime, a seemingly innocuous or familiar thought can also pop up and exert its influence over the transition. Aside from this first type of sign, a memory at the moment of death can appear as a symbol rather than as a recollection of the volitional act itself; for instance, we might see the implement used to commit a deed or the color of an object where that deed was performed. This sort of phenomenon arising in the mind can also inform the particularities of our passage. The third possible predominant mental experience at the moment of death pertains to what is called "destination," and it is considered a portent of characteristics that the dying person might encounter.

Regardless of what arises, what matters is not the image but how it is processed within the heart of the dying person. This means our words and guidance can to some degree benefit the last mind-moment of another practitioner.

If a dying person's mind is totally suffused with impermanence, then the most prominent factor dominating their mind in the last thought sequence is impermanence. If impermanence is the only salient feature in our mind when we die, then it follows that our patterning cannot and does not find any permanent landing place—human or divine realm— to which it can adhere, or in which to be reborn. There is no perpetuation. When the mind no longer sticks to any familiar signpost, there is freedom.

All defilements are "given up, cut off at the root, made like a palm stump, and obliterated, so that they are unable to arise in the future."[82] The unshakable heart's release is said to be the best kind of signless heart's release. Of this release, its mode is said to be signlessness, for when impermanence is known completely, the heart is completely emptied of greed, hatred, and delusion. They were only architects of signs to which we clung or which we resisted. The peace that ensues is therefore unshakable and lasting. In touching deeply into impermanence, we touch the limitless, the unconditioned, nibbana.

Acknowledgments

Our gratitude goes to Jeanne Malmgren, coeditor of *Journey to Mindfulness*, for her initial work on this project. When Jeff Geason, office manager at the Bhavana Society, met Julia Harris through the world of Dhamma writing and editing, the miracle of connectedness led him to introduce her to Bhante Gunaratana. Jeff and Brian Chamowitz, Bhante's excellent helper of many hats, welcomed Julia into their sphere in ways that made for mutual harmony and this book. Bhante extends his special thanks to Julia for working painstakingly to edit, coauthor, and polish the voice of this manuscript. Julia delights in Bhante's trusting invitation to do so. We applaud Laura Cunningham, editorial and production manager at Wisdom Publications, and Michael Butcher, editorial assistant, for their exceptional communication skills and for coordinating preparations for publication. We thank Jeff for proofreading the manuscript and Richard Zeikowitz for checking citations in the *Anguttara Nikaya* and *Suttanipata*. Julia wishes to recognize her neighbor Denise for looking up page numbers in her personal copy of the *Dhammapada*. We express our collective appreciation to Wisdom Publications for their very fine way of presenting the book to our readers.

Abbreviations for Pali Sutta Citations

AN   *Anguttara Nikaya*
Dhp   *Dhammapada*
DhpA   *Dhammapada-atthakatha*
DN   *Digha Nikaya*
MN   *Majjhima Nikaya*
SN   *Samyutta Nikaya*
Sn   *Suttanipata*
Ud   *Udana*

Notes

1. DN 26. Mara is a tricky character to be discussed later in this chapter.
2. SN 22:43.
3. SN 6:2.
4. SN 6:2.
5. SN 22:87.
6. SN 47:20; Bodhi 2000, 1649.
7. SN 35:70; Bodhi 2000, 1155.
8. DN 22.
9. MN 10; Ñāṇamoli and Bodhi 1995, 151.
10. MN 10; Ñāṇamoli and Bodhi 1995, 153.
11. MN 10; Ñāṇamoli and Bodhi 1995, 153–54.
12. MN 131; Ñāṇamoli and Bodhi 1995, 1045.
13. SN 12.61.
14. SN 1:1. To learn more about the four types of floods described by the Buddha, namely sensual desire, the urge for becoming, fixed views, and ignorance, see also the *Ogha Sutta, Floods,* SN 45.171.
15. SN 47:6; Bodhi 2000, 1632–33.
16. Ud 1:10; Ireland 1997, 21.
17. Sn 3:12; Bodhi 2017, 756–58.
18. *Namuci* is an epithet for death, the destroyer; his name evokes the image of humans and gods alike struggling to escape his grasp.
19. Sn 3:2; Bodhi 2017, 436–39.
20. SN 22:102; Bodhi 2000, 961–62.
21. SN 56:11.
22. SN 22:59. An arahant is someone whose mind and heart are free of all greed, aversion, and confusion. Arahantship is one of three varieties of enlightenment to which Theravada Buddhists may aspire.
23. The five aggregates subject to clinging (*panc-upadana-khanda*) include form, such as raw sense inputs and mere thoughts; feeling, including sensations of pleasant, unpleasant, or neither-pleasant-nor-unpleasant; perception, involved with memory and identification of phenomena; mental proliferation along with volitional formations; and consciousness.
24. MN 146; Ñāṇamoli and Bodhi 1995, 1121.
25. SN 22:29; Bodhi 2000, 875–76.
26. SN 22:31; Bodhi 2000, 876.
27. DN 15.

28. SN 56:11.
29. Dhp 165; Fronsdal 2005, 44.
30. Dhp 240; Fronsdal 2005, 63.
31. Dhp 259.
32. DN 22.
33. SN 10:12.
34. Khandas are aggregates or clusters of sensory data and their mental reverberations that might erroneously be construed as a self. This will be covered further in chapter 8 in relation to the five aggregates.
35. Dhp 374; Fronsdal 2005, 75.
36. Samsara is the inherently painful state of doing things over and over again and never being quite satisfied, like a hamster on a wheel that thinks it is going somewhere. In Buddhist meditation this even applies to entire lifetimes.
37. An active sankhara is one variety of khanda; it denotes a cluster of sensory or mental data that we easily fall for, believing each cluster to be a real and discrete entity. Sankharas are built upon unconscious contact at any sense door or the mind and are the ensuing mental proliferation that arises out of unrecognized feeling. Since kammas are intentional actions that have real effects, they themselves are sankharas, and they can generate more clustering in turn. Both new kammas, such as volition, and old resultant kammas, like your current state, are sankharas.
38. One day a friend of mine came to the Bhavana Society, and during casual conversation with me and the other residents he jokingly asked us the meaning of a word he coined: "'On' and 'on,' with 'I' in the middle." We used all of our knowledge and wit to try to solve this riddle, but we could not. Finally he spelled it out and said, "Onion," and we all laughed. Later on I began to think about this riddle. I saw that it makes perfect sense if you think about the way we go on and on in samsara, because craving and ignorance are constantly supporting the notion of "I."
39. Dhp 294–95; Fronsdal 2005, 75.
40. SN 22:59; Bodhi 2000, 901–2.
41. SN 22:1; Bodhi 2000, 853–56.
42. MN 2; Ñāṇamoli and Bodhi 1995, 93.
43. MN 131.
44. DhpA III 406–7.
45. DhpA III 417–21.
46. DN 16.
47. Gunaratana 2012, 113.
48. AN 4:45; Bodhi 2012, 434–35.
49. AN 11:16 (in other editions AN 11:15, for instance in Bodhi 2012, 1573–74).
50. AN 10:58.
51. SN 35:28.
52. *Jatiya jara-maranena soka-parideva-dukkha-domanass'upayasapi dukkha*, a stock phrase and good reminder from the Pali canonical texts.
53. SN 22:87.
54. AN 11:16 (in other editions AN 11:15, for instance in Bodhi 2012, 1573–74).
55. Ibid.
56. Ibid.

57. Sn 143–45.
58. AN 10.13.
59. Later Buddhist traditions enumerate ten stages leading up to buddhahood.
60. An epithet for the Buddha, meaning "Thus gone one" or "Thus come one."
61. A "solitary buddha."
62. A word for the Buddha's teaching, dispensed as a healing medicine for those who suffer.
63. MN 142; Ñāṇamoli and Bodhi 1995: 1103–4.
64. MN 63.
65. AN 2:19.
66. Dhp 183.
67. SN 35:97; Bodhi 2000, 1179–80.
68. MN 152; Ñāṇamoli and Bodhi 1995: 1148–49.
69. SN 35:99.
70. SN 22:102.
71. AN 3:65; Bodhi 2012, 279–83.
72. AN 4,180 (DN 16).
73. *Matika* refers to an itemized index of phenomena as understood in early Buddhist practice and theory. This Pali word connotes a sort of matrix for recognizing and unbinding things that occur within subtle layers of mind.
74. MN 52. See also the *Anupada Sutta, The Discourse on One by One* (or *One After Another*), MN 111.
75. MN 111; Ñāṇamoli and Bodhi 1995: 899.
76. Ibid.
77. MN 149; Ñāṇamoli and Bodhi 1995: 1138–39.
78. SN 35:99.
79. AN 8:73; Bodhi 2012, 1219–21.
80. MN 118; Ñāṇamoli and Bodhi 1995: 83.
81. AN 10:58.
82. MN 43.

Bibliography

Bodhi, Bhikkhu, trans. *The Connected Discourses of the Buddha: A Translation of the Saṃyutta Nikāya.* Boston: Wisdom Publications, 2000.

———. *The Numerical Discourses of the Buddha: A Translation of the Aṅguttara Nikāya.* Boston: Wisdom Publications, 2012.

———. *The Suttanipāta: An Ancient Collection of the Buddha's Discourses Together with Its Commentaries.* Boston: Wisdom Publications, 2017.

Buddhaghosa. *The Buddha's Last Days: Buddhaghosa's Commentary on the Mahaparinibbana Sutta.* Translated by Yang-gyu An. Oxford: Pali Text Society, 2003.

———. *The Commentary on the Dhammapada.* Vol. 3. Edited by H. C. Norman. London: Luzac & Company, Ltd. 1970.

Fronsdal, Gil, trans. *The Dhammapada: A New Translation of the Buddhist Classic with Annotations.* Boston & London: Shambhala Publications, 2005.

Gunaratana, Henepola. *The Four Foundations of Mindfulness in Plain English.* Boston: Wisdom Publications, 2012.

Ireland, John D., trans. *The Udāna: Inspired Utterances of the Buddha & The Itivuttaka: The Buddha's Sayings.* Kandy, Sri Lanka: Buddhist Publication Society, 1997.

Ñāṇamoli, Bhikkhu, and Bhikkhu Bodhi, trans. *The Middle Length Discourses of the Buddha.* Boston: Wisdom Publications, 1995.

Nārada Mahā Thera, Venerable. *The Buddha and His Teachings.* Kandy, Sri Lanka: Buddhist Publication Society, 1988.

Walshe, Maurice, trans. *The Long Discourses of the Buddha: A Translation of the Dīgha Nikāya.* Boston: Wisdom Publications, 1987.

Woodward, F. L., trans. *The Book of the Gradual Sayings (Aṅguttara-Nikāya) or More-numbered Suttas.* Oxford: Pāli Text Society, 2003.

About the Authors

BHANTE GUNARATANA was ordained at the age of twelve as a Buddhist monk in Sri Lanka, earned his PhD in philosophy from American University, and has led meditation retreats, taught Buddhism, and lectured widely throughout the United States, Canada, Europe, and Australia. Bhante Henepola Gunaratana is the president of the Bhavana Society in High View, West Virginia, where he lives.

JULIA HARRIS lives and meditates in Colorado, though the mind still roams far beyond the mountains of her home. If even one reader relaxes the ties of personality view and conceptual elaboration by reading this book, her heart will rejoice.

What to Read Next from Wisdom Publications

Mindfulness in Plain English
Bhante Gunaratana

"A classic—one of the very best English sources for authoritative explanations of mindfulness."—Daniel Goleman, author of *Emotional Intelligence*

Start Here, Start Now
A Short Guide to Mindfulness Meditation
Bhante Gunaratana

"A timeless, clear, and beautiful introduction."—Tamara Levitt, Head of Mindfulness at Calm

Eight Mindful Steps to Happiness
Walking the Buddha's Path
Bhante Gunaratana

"An astoundingly clear and joyful guide to living life at the deepest level."—*Inquiring Mind*

What, Why, How
Bhante Gunaratana

"This book can be of help to anyone's spiritual journey and meditation practice."—Sharon Salzberg, author of *Lovingkindness* and *Real Happiness*

Beyond Mindfulness in Plain English
An Introductory Guide to Deeper States of Meditation
Bhante Gunaratana

"Bhante Gunaratana has done it again! There is practical logic and an almost startling common sense to the explanations that lead the reader smoothly through the various stages of meditative concentration."
—Ajahn Amaro, abbot of Abhayagiri Monastery

Loving-Kindness in Plain English
The Practice of Metta
Bhante Gunaratana

"This beautiful book not only expertly guides us in cultivating loving-kindness, it is the transmission of an awakened heart. Bhante G, as he is affectionately called, is a true master, and his deep wisdom and love flow through his words into our hearts. Written with great lucidity, and filled with accessible, powerful teachings and practices, *Loving-Kindness in Plain English* is a book that will bring more love into your life."
—Tara Brach, PhD, author of *Radical Acceptance* and *True Refuge*

Beyond Distraction
Five Practical Ways to Focus the Mind
Shaila Catherine

This book contains a wealth of pragmatic advice for both new and experienced meditators, and it will be an invaluable guide for all those journeying on the path to greater freedom."—Joseph Goldstein, author of *Mindfulness: A Practical Guide to Awakening*

Emptiness

A Practical Guide for Meditators

Guy Armstrong

In this book, Guy Armstrong makes difficult Buddhist topics easy to understand, weaving together Theravada and Mahayana teachings on emptiness to show how we can liberate our minds and manifest compassion in our lives.

About Wisdom Publications

Wisdom Publications is the leading publisher of classic and contemporary Buddhist books and practical works on mindfulness. To learn more about us or to explore our other books, please visit our website at wisdomexperience.org or contact us at the address below.

Wisdom Publications
132 Perry Street
New York, NY 10014 USA

We are a 501(c)(3) organization, and donations in support of our mission are tax deductible.

Wisdom Publications is affiliated with the Foundation for the Preservation of the Mahayana Tradition (FPMT).